The Best Loved Trees of America

The Best Loved

BY THE FORMER MANAGING EDITOR OF

Garden City, New York

Trees of America

INTIMATE CLOSE-UPS OF THEIR YEAR-ROUND TRAITS

The Home Garden: ROBERT S. LEMMON

The American Garden Guild and Doubleday & Company, Inc.

DEDICATED TO EVERYONE
WHO FEELS THE MAJESTY AND MYSTERY OF TREES

INTRODUCTION

From the dawn of human history men have worshiped trees, for even in the earliest days the influences of the forests were as vital in their lives as those of the sun and rain, the winds, the waters and the plains and mountains. Shade from summer's heat, refuge in time of storm, wood for fuel and food for the body, weapons, utensils, family shelter, craft to journey along the water-ways—all these were creature needs that only trees could satisfy. Out of their fulfillment there grew in Man a sense of gratitude, of veneration, that in time became all but instinctive. Even today, amid the confusions and complexities of our modern world, we are all potential tree worshipers at heart, whether we realize it or not.

It is upon the foundation of this age-old attachment of men for trees that the present book was built. As you will soon discover, it is not essentially a volume on how to grow trees or identify them, although it contains much information pointing in those directions. Nor is it a mere flight of fancy, despite its occasional tendency to follow byways that have only tenuous connection with the living realities of roots and trunks and branches. Certainly you could not call it a summary of American trees, for there are many kinds which it does not mention. If it must be given a classification, perhaps you should think of it as a book of tree appreciation, written in the hope that here and there, as you turn its pages, you will come upon a thought or phrase or picture that will stir a responsive chord quite deep within you.

Implementation of the plan which is now before you in completed form began in 1945 and continued until the spring of 1951. At the start I intended to include only species indigenous to the United States—original Americans, if you will. Subsequently, however, it seemed best to make an exception to this rule by admitting the Horse-chestnut, simply because, although it originated in Europe, it has spread so widely in America and has been so well loved by successive generations that for all practical purposes it is a true native.

Once the list of trees to be covered had been settled after many conferences and much correspondence with tree-knowing folk in various parts of the country, there came the problem of finding photographers with the necessary skill and sympathy for trees to take the special sort of pictures which were so essential to the plan. In this I was particularly fortunate. Theirs was no easy assignment, for upon them fell the bulk of the task of locating typical specimens of the desired species growing in situations where a camera lens could capture not only their full figures but also their personalities and at least a suggestion of the spirit of their natural surroundings. Furthermore, many of the trees selected had to be visited at least twice, in order to photograph them from the same spot in their winter as well as summer dress, and to collect the flower, leaf, and fruit details which had to be brought back and photographed close-up in the studio against a background usually of 1-inch squares as a key to their respective sizes.

My thanks and sincere appreciation go to all these patient cameramen who played their parts so well. Especially am I grateful for having had, from the outset, the close co-operation, understanding, and enthusiasm of Samuel H. Gottscho and William Schleisner, many of whose superb photographs are reproduced on subsequent pages. Indeed, if it had not been for Mr. Gottscho, this book might never have been undertaken, for it was he who first suggested the general theme on which it has been developed.

R.S.L.

CONTENTS
AND ILLUSTRATIONS

7   Introduction

16   Monterey Pine, *Pinus radiata*
     SUMNER FROM MONKMEYER

20   Bull Bay, *Magnolia grandiflora*
     WATSON FROM MONKMEYER

24   American Beech, *Fagus sylvatica*
     GOTTSCHO-SCHLEISNER

28   Red-cedar, *Juniperus virginiana*
     GOTTSCHO-SCHLEISNER

32   Red Maple, *Acer rubrum*
     GOTTSCHO-SCHLEISNER

37   Sycamore, *Platanus occidentalis*
     GOTTSCHO-SCHLEISNER

41   Sugar Pine, *Pinus Lambertiana*
     SUMNER FROM MONKMEYER

46   Sweet Gum, *Liquidambar styraciflua*
     GOTTSCHO-SCHLEISNER

50   Northern Red Oak, *Quercus borealis*
     GOTTSCHO-SCHLEISNER

54   Sassafras, *Sassafras variifolium*
     GOTTSCHO-SCHLEISNER

59   White Pine, *Pinus strobus*
     GOTTSCHO-SCHLEISNER

62   White Oak, *Quercus alba*
     GOTTSCHO-SCHLEISNER

65   Black Locust, *Robinia pseudoacacia*
     GOTTSCHO-SCHLEISNER

69   Black Spruce, *Picea mariana*
     GOTTSCHO-SCHLEISNER

72   White Ash, *Fraxinus americana*
     GOTTSCHO-SCHLEISNER

76   Shagbark Hickory, *Carya ovata*
     GOTTSCHO-SCHLEISNER

80   Hemlock, *Tsuga canadensis*
     GOTTSCHO-SCHLEISNER

83   Tulip-tree, *Liriodendron tulipifera*
     GOTTSCHO-SCHLEISNER

88   Pin Oak, *Quercus palustris*
     GOTTSCHO-SCHLEISNER

91   Black Walnut, *Juglans nigra*
     GOTTSCHO-SCHLEISNER

97   Pecan, *Carya pecan*
     WATSON FROM MONKMEYER

101 Sugar Maple, *Acer saccharum*
     GOTTSCHO-SCHLEISNER

105 Black Oak, *Quercus velutina*
     GOTTSCHO-SCHLEISNER

108 Giant Sequoia, *Sequoiadendron gigantea*
     SUMNER FROM MONKMEYER

112 Persimmon, *Diospyros virginiana*
     WATSON FROM MONKMEYER

116 American Elm, *Ulmus americana*
     GOTTSCHO-SCHLEISNER

120   Pepperidge, *Nyssa sylvatica*
RICHARD AVERILL SMITH; GOTTSCHO-SCHLEISNER

124   Western Juniper, *Juniperus occidentalis*
SUMNER FROM MONKMEYER

128   California Live Oak, *Quercus chrysolepis*
SUMNER FROM MONKMEYER

132   Douglas-fir, *Pseudotsuga taxifolia*
SUMNER FROM MONKMEYER

136   Flowering Dogwood, *Cornus florida*
GOTTSCHO-SCHLEISNER

144   Long-leaf Pine, *Pinus palustris*
WATSON FROM MONKMEYER

148   Cottonwood, *Populus deltoidea*
GOTTSCHO-SCHLEISNER; J. H. MCFARLAND

152   Willow Oak, *Quercus phellos*
WATSON FROM MONKMEYER

155   Horse-chestnut, *Aesculus hippocastanum*
WATSON FROM MONKMEYER

158   Ponderosa Pine, *Pinus ponderosa*
SUMNER FROM MONKMEYER; STEENSON AND BAKER

162   California Buckeye, *Aesculus californica*
SUMNER FROM MONKMEYER

165   Incense-cedar, *Libocedrus decurrens*
SUMNER FROM MONKMEYER

168   California-laurel, *Umbellularia californica*
SUMNER FROM MONKMEYER

171   Live Oak, *Quercus virginiana*
WATSON FROM MONKMEYER

11

175   Monterey Cypress, *Cupressus macrocarpa*
SUMNER FROM MONKMEYER

178   Fremont Cottonwood, *Populus Fremonti*
SUMNER FROM MONKMEYER; GERARD FROM MONKMEYER

181   American Holly, *Ilex opaca*
WATSON FROM MONKMEYER

184   Canoe Birch, *Betulus papyrifera*
STEENSON AND BAKER

188   Coast Redwood, *Sequoia sempervirens*
SUMNER FROM MONKMEYER

192   Joshua-tree, *Yucca brevifolia*
SUMNER FROM MONKMEYER

196   Washington Palm, *Washingtonia filifera*
SUMNER FROM MONKMEYER

200   Gray Birch, *Betulus populifolia*
STEENSON AND BAKER

204   Mountain Hemlock, *Tsuga Mertensiana*
SUMNER FROM MONKMEYER

208   American Linden, *Tilia americana*
GOTTSCHO-SCHLEISNER

212   Torrey Pine, *Pinus Torreyana*
SUMNER FROM MONKMEYER

216   Palo Verde, *Cercidium Torreyanum*
SUMNER FROM MONKMEYER

220   Cucumber-tree, *Magnolia acuminata*
STEENSON AND BAKER

223   California Black Oak, *Quercus Kelloggi*
SUMNER FROM MONKMEYER

12

227 Honey Locust, *Gleditsia triacanthos*
        GOTTSCHO-SCHLEISNER

233 White Fir, *Abies concolor*
        SUMNER FROM MONKMEYER

236 White-cedar, *Chamaecyparis thyoides*
        GOTTSCHO-SCHLEISNER

239 American Mountain-ash, *Sorbus americana*
        GOTTSCHO-SCHLEISNER

243 Pignut Hickory, *Carya glabra*
        GOTTSCHO-SCHLEISNER

249 Index

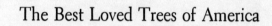

The Best Loved Trees of America

MONTEREY
PINE

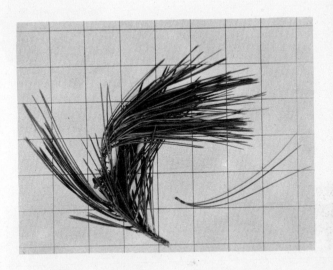

California is a remarkable state in many respects, but to numerous lovers of our native trees one of its most outstanding features is the variety of indigenous species which are extremely local in distribution. Take, for example, the Monterey Pine (*Pinus radiata*). This tree, as its name suggests, is found on the Monterey Peninsula, southward at intervals along the coast as far as Santa Rosa and Santa Cruz Islands, and Guadalupe Island off Lower California. Fortunately it has also been introduced northward along the coast to Vancouver Island, as well as into parts of our own South and into southern and western Europe, so the prospects are that as a species it does not face extinction, regardless of whatever may happen to its limited native habitat.

When happily situated, Monterey Pines grow to be big fellows —sometimes as much as 100 feet tall, and 5 feet thick at the butt. Their wood is rather soft and weak, though, so that with age, and in a position exposed to heavy winds, branch breakage may lead

to the sort of fantastic effect presented by the old fellow in the accompanying photograph. Normally the form of a mature tree is broadly spreading (there's a glimpse of one in the background of the photograph), but even a wind-battered veteran like this one shows clearly the density of the mass of grass-green foliage which is so characteristic of the species. These needles, from 4 to 6 inches long, are usually grouped in bundles of three, sometimes two. Though they persist no longer than three years, the tree is always well furnished with bright new ones whose silvery sheen helps to keep it handsome and fresh-looking.

In a suitably mild climate, such as that of the Pacific coast, the Monterey Pine is a thoroughly satisfactory ornamental and reforesting tree, handsome and fast-growing, with picturesquely rough sepia brown or even blackish bark and long-lasting cones up to 5 inches in length. Actually, these cones often do not shed their seeds for several years, and it is customary for the cones themselves to remain on the tree for ten years or more, finally becoming imbedded in the growth of the twigs which produced them. Remember, though, that this tree is unlikely to survive where winters are severe.

Like all Pines, the Monterey is at its best in an open, uncrowded spot where it has plenty of room to develop its generous, well-filled form. While young it looks almost bushy, and traces of this character show even at maturity. It is especially good for seaside planting, as might be expected from the environment of its native home. Incidentally, proximity to salt water considerably extends the range of territory in which it can be expected to prove hardy, for coastal areas are almost invariably warmer in winter than are corresponding ones even just a few miles inland.

Monterey Pines follow the predominant family tradition of preferring sandy, well-drained soil which is poor rather than rich in plant nutrients; their root systems are geared to lean fare, apparently, and providing them with generous food and drink is likely to have adverse effects. However, during transplanting operations it is exceptionally important to guard against the slightest drying of these same roots, so be lavish with burlap coverings and the use of water. Early spring is the best moving time, except in regions with hot, dry summers. Under the latter conditions autumn is preferable.

BULL BAY

The scientists call it *Magnolia grandiflora*, while to less technical folk it may be Large-flowered Magnolia or simply Bull Bay. Not even a dozen names, though, could confuse its identity or lessen its prestige as one of the truly great trees of the Deep South. Completely evergreen, majestic in stature, superb in the beauty and fragrance of its 8-inch creamy-white blossoms in their setting of lustrous dark leaves with rusty down on the underside, the Bull Bay richly deserves its chapter in this book.

The South is our real Magnolia Country. It is there—from the coast region of lower North Carolina along the Atlantic coast to Florida and west through the Gulf States to the Brazos River in Texas, as well as through western Louisiana to the lower part of Arkansas—that the Bull Bay towers 50, 70, or even 90 feet above the rich alluvial soil of the lowlands. At its best it is a broad, dense pyramid of gray-brown trunk and boughs clothed with countless 5- to 8-inch leathery leaves to which the flowers give the crowning waterlily-like touch in April or May. After the flowers have gone by you notice the first development stages of the odd-looking fruit— dull rose pink changing to tannish brown as it approaches its mature length of 3 inches or so. When fully ripe the numerous individual pods of the fruit split open and from each one a showy coral-red seed emerges and hangs for a time by a slender thread— a favorite Magnolia habit of which one never tires.

Within the region where it can be grown, the Bull Bay is in the front rank of large ornamental flowering trees, especially for an open, uncrowded spot where it can develop its normal, well-filled form. Outside of its natural range it is likely to withstand the winter as far north as Washington, except in the mountain regions. Beyond that point I'd hesitate to recommend its planting, though the experiment might work here and there. After all, this whole question of the hardiness of trees outside of their natural habitat is one to which only a reckless or ignorant man would care to give a flat yes-or-no answer.

As such things go, the Bull Bay is quite free from bug troubles. The chief pests to watch for are scale insects of various kinds, notably the Magnolia and Tulip-tree scales. Infestation is not likely to be serious, though, and the control measures are fairly simple—dormant oil spray in winter or very early spring for the hard-shelled types of scale, and white oil sprays in summer for the soft ones.

Just about any good loamy soil, preferably on the dampish side, will suit this front-rank member of the Magnolia clan. As transplanting of good-sized specimens is likely to be a precarious business, the safest course is to move only little fellows and try to school yourself in patience while they're growing up. Early spring is the most favorable season, and nursery-grown trees hold the most promise of success.

AMERICAN
BEECH

From Nova Scotia westward to Michigan and Wisconsin and south all the way to upper Florida this Beech (*Fagus sylvatica*) is among the most notable of our larger forest trees. Typically it is quite wide-spreading and round-topped, and it is no unusual matter to come upon one a good 75 or 80 feet tall, with a trunk butt 3 feet thick.

A well-grown Beech is sturdy refinement personified. At very first glance you are impressed by the beauty of the bark that clothes its trunk and limbs in smooth, light gray, finely speckled and occasionally blotched with darker tones so that the mass pattern is wonderfully intricate and varied. Out among the myriad slender, angled twigs this smoothness is even more pronounced, and the pale color more uniform though more inclined to brownish. The whole tree seems the perfect framework for the countless flat sprays of thin, straight-veined leaves which, pure light green when they burst their long, slender coverings in spring, persist as pale buff wraiths far into the following winter. It is no unusual experience, when walking in the otherwise bare December woods, to see the Beech branches curiously clothed in mingled snow and withered but still attractive leaves, the latter rustling softly as the wind marches past.

This is the tree whose odd little three-sided nuts, nested always in pairs inside minute burrs, are such an important food item for the woods creatures—mice, jays, squirrels, and, in those regions where it still roams, the superb wild turkey. Indeed, many a forest-wise human nibbles them with relish, for they are undeniably sweet and tasty. Why they should be so abundantly borne every third or fourth year, and scarce betweentimes, is for better naturalists than I to answer.

I never see a big Beech without recalling how, as boys, we used to search the more or less horizontal branches for hummingbirds' nests. In our section, at least, the tiny darting jewels seemed to prefer this tree to all others, and we used to follow their bullet flight from the honeysuckles around the house veranda until, hav-

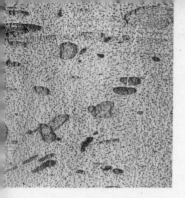

ing determined the general direction, we could pick it up at successive points along the line and eventually, more often than not, fix its destination in some one of the several large Beeches in the nearby woods. Then we would lie on our backs under the tree (that was easier on our necks, you see) and patiently study the smaller branches far above until, aided by momentary glimpses of the hummer itself, we located the slight swelling on the branch which was the nest. Yes, it called for sharp eyes—young country eyes—and a certain love of the game for its own sake. But it was fun!

Beeches like rich, well-drained but not parched ground, and though, as mentioned before, they are naturally woodland trees, they will do splendidly as specimens in the full open. One could hardly recommend them for planting on most small properties, simply because of their great stature which comes with the passing years. But where there is space commensurate with their natural size they rank among the best of shade-type ornamentals, whether native American or imported. From my observation they are about as pest- and disease-free as any tree you are likely to find.

Transplanting an American Beech from the wild is a risky operation; anyone who can succeed in it with any consistency is either a genius or a special pet of the gods of chance. If you do try it, be sure to choose a very small one that has grown in a rockless spot where a job of real root digging can be done. Fortunately, nursery-grown trees in the smaller sizes are less of a headache and are always to be preferred if a source of supply is reasonably near at hand. As between fall and spring moving, I doubt if there is much to choose. In either case careful attention to watering until strong new growth shows that the roots have really taken hold is highly important.

26

27

RED-CEDAR

Among our native evergreens the Red-cedar (*Juniperus virginiana*) seems somehow closest to the everyday lives of everyday folk, young and old. It is a friendly sort of tree, a lover of pasture hills and farm hedgerows, happy in the broad, free spaces of the open country where sun and wind have full play through the heat of summer and when the land is overlaid with snow. Only rarely do you find it hidden in the woods, and when you do it is no more than a straggly, ill-featured caricature of its normal sturdy self. True American that it is, you will meet it from New Brunswick to the Dakotas and southward all the way to Texas and northern Florida. The Texas region provides perhaps its most favorable home, for there it may reach a height of 90 feet with a trunk diameter of 4 or 5—at least double the stature it is likely to attain in the North.

Few evergreens are as variable in form and color as the Red-

cedar. As a rule it is slender and column-like in youth and early middle age—sometimes as narrow as 3 feet despite a height of 25. Again, you will see dozens in a colony, every one superbly dense and symmetrical, while a half mile away the prevailing type may be so loose in its branching that you can look through the foliage and see the sky at almost any point. Only with age does the somewhat pyramidal form develop, such as that in the present photograph.

The prevailing color is a darkish, somewhat dull green, but individual trees sometimes are uniformly a bright, almost grass green, while occasionally one will have a definitely bluish or silvery cast. I have never seen any variation, though, in the color of the often numerous little "berries," a few of which show in the right-hand part of the detail photograph of a branch tip; at first they are pale grayish green, turning to light silvery or cadet blue in autumn. I suspect that many kinds of birds find them welcome food when the weather grows chilly; certainly the robins do, and of course it is his fondness for the tree—as a restaurant no less than for a nesting site—that gives the cedar waxwing his common name.

Another peculiarity is the two types of "leaves" which young trees, and occasionally older ones, normally carry. One, known as the juvenile form, is sharp-pointed and needle-like, as in the case of the allied lower-growing junipers, while the other is rounded and overlapping, somewhat suggestive of an Arborvitae but lacking the latter's flat, fan-like character. As the tree grows older the needle leaves customarily disappear entirely, being replaced by the distinctive somewhat tufty form. In very young trees, too, the bark is likely to be rather scaly or plate-like in appearance, but this soon changes to a light brown shreddy surface which, if you are experimentally inclined, can be pulled off in long, soft strips.

Internally, perhaps the most noteworthy feature of the Red-cedar is its soft, close-grained wood, fragrant as incense and, to my mind, far more pleasing as a scent than that famous commodity. This is the brownish-red, often white-figured wood employed for cedar chests and closets, for pencils, for interior paneling, household utensils, and many other everyday purposes. Despite its softness it is remarkably resistant to rot and therefore famous as a material for long-lasting fence posts, shingles, and the like.

Red-cedars are capable of excellent home landscape effects, especially as background plantings and tall accent points. They are a bit hard to transplant, though, even when nursery-grown, and it is advisable to move them only when small—under 6 feet in height, if possible. Their chief drawback—and a most important one—is that they are the chosen intermediate host plant for the serious apple-rust disease, a fact which leads to their virtual banning in some regions where apple growing is an important project.

RED MAPLE

Every now and then the folk who think up names for plants hit upon an appellation so clearly appropriate that one welcomes its simplicity and significance with almost a sigh of relief. One such instance is the White Birch, and another is the Weeping Willow. For a third—and a peculiarly satisfying third, at that—there's the Red Maple (*Acer rubrum*).

There are no more than two or three months in the year when this handsome tree fails to prove its right to be called "red." In earliest spring its buds begin to turn from their dull maroon winter color to a brighter, lighter hue that grows more and more intense until, when the blossoms actually open, the whole tree seems to glow in the pale sunshine. The same red is in the opening leaves and the winged seeds and tinges the twigs and leaf stems all summer. When the autumn color show sweeps across the countryside the Red Maple is perhaps its most brilliant, almost startlingly conspicuous entry. Even after winter closes in, the tone is not wholly lost, but lingers in the younger bark and buds as though merely waiting for the day when it can flame out again.

33

Red Maples are very widely distributed trees, growing naturally from Nova Scotia west through Quebec and Ontario to Lake of the Woods, the Dakotas and Nebraska, and south into Texas and Florida. Evidently the trees are exceptionally adaptable to variations in temperature as well as other climatic factors, for they are found even well up into the mountains of northern New England, where the winter cold is, of course, more intense than the mere geographical location would indicate. On the underground side of the picture they seem to prefer damp or actually wet soil conditions; hence the other common names of Swamp Maple and Water Maple. You'll find many a one, though, that has been planted in an average well-drained spot and seems entirely happy about it.

This Maple isn't by any means a giant, as trees go—from 40- to 50-odd feet is about as tall as it is likely to become, except in woods where the competition to reach up into the sunlight may cause it to attain greater height. In contour, as the photographs show, it looks not unlike the Sugar Maple, but as a rule the branch habit is

34

sufficiently different from that of the Sugar to be a helpful mark of distinction when one is fairly familiar with both trees. The bark is smooth and a light brownish gray on young trees, but very dark, furrowed, and often shaggy on old ones.

Red Maples are good home-grounds shade trees, but it must be remembered that, like other members of the genus, they pose a problem of how to keep lawn grass happy underneath them when they have attained considerable size. Normally they are well-formed and shapely, high-branched rather than low, quite resistant to storm breakage, and no more subject to serious insect or disease headaches than dozens of other kinds of trees. Incidentally, it may be noted in passing that this species is frequently tapped for the making of those delectable sweets which are called "maple products" up New England way. Along with the Sugar or Rock Maple (*Acer saccharum*) especially, and the White or Silver Maple (*Acer saccharinum*), the Red contributes to the sap-boiling industry and is said to yield as good a percentage of sugar as any of the others.

In planting one of these trees on the home grounds it is desirable, of course, to select a spot where ample space will allow it to develop its normal symmetry and also to be seen in full effectiveness. Autumn is the best transplanting season, for Red Maples start growth activity so early in the spring that it's hard to move them then without upsetting their calculations considerably. As with all trees, nursery-grown individuals are easier than wild ones and as a rule are better shaped too. In making a selection, look for one that is straight in the trunk and evenly branched on all sides. Be cautious of the tree that has been crowded in the nursery row, for it may not develop its true form for a long time. The best size to buy depends a good deal on how much you feel like paying, but as a general rule get one that is between 8 and 12 feet high. Be sure to keep it heavily watered during dry times throughout the first full year in the new location—even longer than that if a severe drought develops.

In the accompanying detail photograph of the Red Maple's leaves, as in similar illustrations in this book, each of the small squares which compose the background represents an area of 1 inch. With this as a guide, the calculation of the actual size of leaf, flower, or fruit is simple.

SYCAMORE

By whichever of its common names one calls it—Buttonball, Buttonwood, Plane-tree, Sycamore—this handsome, picturesque giant is an outstanding feature of many a country and suburban scene from Maine to Ontario and Minnesota, and south to Florida and Texas. Its natural range is nearly as large as that of the American Elm, and its stature is even greater—as much as 170 feet sometimes. Some authorities even rate it as the tallest-growing of all the deciduous trees native to this country. Scientific folk call it *Platanus occidentalis,* thus distinguishing it from several related species in the Old World.

To say that the Sycamore is massive suggests only one of the several characteristics which give it outstanding prominence. The bark at the base of its trunk is dark brown and rather deeply fissured, but on the limbs and far up among the branches the bark is a curiously mottled mixture of smooth creamy-white blotches and darker, older areas where the characteristic "peeling" process has not yet commenced. In summer, when the huge, deeply lobed leaves convert the whole tree into a mighty pile of green, this odd appearance of the bark is partially masked; but once autumn has stripped the twigs, the whole framework in its queer dress is as startlingly unique as it is beautiful. After leaf fall, too, one can really see the multi-

tude of little ball-like seed clusters hanging from the twig tips, unfailing memories of many a country childhood.

I have never been able to decide which season of the year shows the Sycamore at its best. In summer it seems as though there could be no finer, more impressive picture of tree majesty and sturdy health—a literal monument to the productive powers of earth and sun and rain. Then, months later, when its mighty form gleams against a windy, deep blue sky, comes the feeling that only now is the picture really perfect. Perhaps the sensible course is just to enjoy it to the full *all* the time!

Generally speaking, Sycamores reach their finest development in fairly low flatlands, for they seem to need a rather constant and ample supply of soil moisture (remember that old song about the candle lights gleaming through the Sycamores on the banks of the Wabash far away?). Seldom do you find a really big one on a hill, though in the meadow near by there may be several. But wherever one stands and whatever its size, you can tell it by its mighty leaves or patchwork bark, or both.

A Sycamore is a good choice where a really large and easily transplanted tree is called for, for it has ample branch spread and its limbs are high enough to admit sufficient light to plants growing underneath it. A deep, rich soil is important. The tree stands pruning well and is strongly resistant to wind and storm damage. However, in certain areas browning of the leaf edge, due to anthracnose, gives the tree a somewhat unsightly appearance during late summer and fall.

Sycamores do not seem to seed very freely, so the chances of your finding a transplantable young tree in the fields or woods are not too good. In most cases it is a matter of buying one from a good nursery—a situation which is doubly advisable inasmuch as nursery-grown trees almost always have better root systems. The best size to buy depends chiefly on what is available and how much you want to pay.

Be sure that the tree you buy is the American Plane (or Sycamore)—not one of the European species, which are quite similar in appearance when small. These foreign kinds are in considerable demand for street and park planting, therefore some nurseries grow them in preference to the American species pictured on these pages.

In the words of the late John Muir, whose knowledge and love of our West Coast forest trees were unsurpassed, the Sugar Pine (*Pinus Lambertiana*) is "The largest, noblest, and most beautiful of all the seventy or eighty species of Pine trees in the world." Sometimes 200 or more feet tall, with a mast-straight trunk that may be 8 or 9 feet thick at the butt, it is a true forest giant whose long, heavy, horizontal limbs are perfectly in keeping with its other proportions. Wide-crowned, and often irregular in its upper outline, the Sugar Pine in the Sierras is surpassed in stature only by the huge members of the Sequoia tribe. Its name, incidentally, derives from the high sugar content of its sap. Wherever one of the trees is wounded, as by an ax, the sap exudes and soon forms crisp, candy-like crystals that taste much like maple sugar.

The seeds, too, are edible by both man and beast. They are borne in enormous cones, sometimes 2 feet long and 4 inches thick, that grow at the ends of the upper branches. Shaped a good deal like those of the White Pine, these monster fruit bearers have 2-inch scales nearly as wide as they are long, brown-tipped and madder purple on their inner surface. For centuries the Indians have eaten

the ripened seeds after they fall to the ground, but the Douglas squirrel is more enterprising in his search for the same food. Even before the cones are mature, he scrabbles up to the tree's top, cuts a cone loose, and scoots back to where it lands on the ground. There, like a small boy conquering an ear of corn, he chisels through the scales to get at the seeds, miraculously keeping his whiskers clear of the gummy substance which permeates the whole cone. It is interesting to note that at least five other West Coast Pines also produce seeds that serve as useful food for humans as well as for animals or birds.

Sugar Pine bark is a dark gray-brown that becomes more reddish on the older trees. Typically its surface is broken into long, irregular, perpendicular plates, at least on the trunk. Underneath it the wood is light, soft, and pale brown and has high commercial value for a variety of lumber purposes. The butt sections, as with most other conifers, are the most nearly free of knots.

This big western Pine belongs to the 5-needle branch of the family—that is, the needles grow in little bundles of five each, whereas some other Pines have only four, three, or even two together. Each

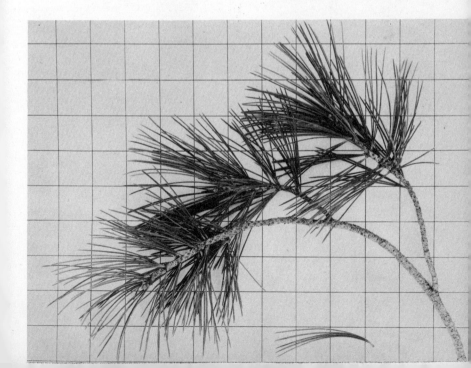

44

needle is fairly thick, from 2¾ to 4 inches long, and the general effect is like that presented by White Pine foliage. The color, however, is a darker green and lacks the White Pine's bluish cast.

The Sugar Pine's native range is from Oregon southward through the Coast and Cascade Ranges and the Sierras to southern and Lower California. It is a reasonably hardy tree in the northeastern states, but if grown there it had better be protected from severe winter winds. Perhaps this is not too important from the landscaping standpoint, for few home properties are spacious enough to accommodate a tree of such massive proportions. And besides, the place to admire Sugar Pine in all its magnificence is in the land of its nativity, where its scale is in keeping with the mountain surroundings and the vastness of the forests.

SWEET
GUM

To anyone who knows the countryside trees from lower New York west and south to Missouri, Arkansas, eastern Oklahoma, northern Florida, and Texas, the Sweet Gum, Liquidambar, or Bilsted, to mention but three of its common names, stands notably apart from all the rest. Not that it is remarkable for size or shape, though on occasion it becomes a giant well over 100 feet tall in the rich, wet lowlands of the Mississippi Basin. Its real distinctiveness, I think, is fourfold: large star-shaped leaves, superb and amazingly varied autumn coloring, odd-looking spherical seed balls which cling to the twigs all winter, and curious cork-like bark ridges along many of the smaller branches. These characteristics, much more than the fact that in the South they make a chewing gum from its resinous sap, account for the right of the Sweet Gum (*Liquidambar styraciflua*) to win a place in this book.

I was a lucky boy to have grown up among Sweet Gums, as it were. At the edge of one of the fields which we boys knew so well, a broad giant with great limbs ranging out and upward in the characteristic rounded form of the species dominated the scene from all directions. On sunny autumn days it was an unbelievable dome of wine red, gold, and purple rising above the surrounding groves of its own seedling offspring. In winter we never tired of wondering why its queer little dark brown seed globes were so different from those of all other trees. When hot June came there was not in all that countryside a pleasanter, more glittering green canopy under which to loaf and nibble the wild strawberries which we had picked in the nearby sunny meadow and strung like beads on leafless stalks of timothy grass. We spoke of it merely as "the big Gum" and were as blissfully ignorant of the origin of that name as of the fact that it was burdened with a scientific designation infinitely longer and more obscure. But I suspect that its beauty and individuality were closer to our hearts and understanding than to those of some older and more enlightened folk.

In view of its many merits and few faults it is a bit hard to understand why the Sweet Gum is so seldom looked upon as a valuable shade and specimen tree for the home grounds. It is not too difficult to transplant, especially if the job is done in early spring, nor does it normally appear to be subject to insect or disease troubles. True, its numerous queer-looking flowers produce rela-

tively few mature seeds—hardly more than two or three in each of its spiny fruiting "balls"—but there would be enough for the nurserymen to build up good stocks of trees if the public wanted them. Possibly there is a prejudice against the cluttering effect of its fallen burrs on the lawn. Or perhaps it's just another instance of familiarity breeding contempt.

From the cultural standpoint, Sweet Gums do their best in rich, rather wet soil, but one often finds entirely satisfactory specimens growing in spots which are definitely on the dry side. One thing the species will not tolerate, though, and that is the relatively cold climate of the northern tier of states. It grows wild rather abundantly along the north shore of Long Island Sound as far east as Fairfield, Connecticut, but ten miles inland from that line one would be lucky to find even a single individual. All in all, my guess is that planting a Sweet Gum in any region where the thermometer is often likely to drop below the zero mark in winter would be a good deal of a gamble. At that, I'd be willing to risk the experiment, just on the chance that it might succeed.

In a way, it seems too bad that a tree of such marked ornamental worth should serve mankind chiefly in ways that are purely utilitarian. Most of us are unaware of the fact that Sweet Gum is the tree that furnishes the close-grained, hard, light brown and buff "gum" wood so admired in house flooring, paneling, and cabinet-making, and less notably used for barrels and woodenware. These, with the use of its sap as a remedy for catarrh and in the making of chewing gum, which has already been mentioned, seem to constitute the chief basis for whatever public fame the Sweet Gum has attained. Perhaps one of these days we will learn to make greater use of the finer, more subtle contributions which it can make as a living, growing entity that gains in beauty as well as in stature throughout the years.

NORTHERN RED OAK

In two respects the Northern Red Oak (*Quercus borealis*) is unique in a tree genus noted for the outstanding character of its members: it extends farther north than any other kind, and it is commonly the tallest of our northern species. You'll find it growing cheerfully far north of New Hampshire's White Mountains and even along the Canadian shore of Lake Huron. Just to prove its adaptability, though, it is also native in Pennsylvania and Iowa. In the matter of dimensions, it ordinarily attains a height of 70 or 80 feet, and in rich woods may reach 140 with a breast-high trunk diameter of 5 to 6 feet. Whatever the dimensions of the tree may be, they present an over-all impression of good proportions. Only when a Red Oak has been badly crowded does it ever look awkward.

Red Oaks follow the family tradition of strength and ruggedness but, especially in woodlands, tend to start their branching farther from the ground than the White and Pin species. The branches, too, while heavy and quite numerous, are irregular and reach upward rather than out, except when a more horizontal direction develops in the case of a tree growing in the open where it does not have to climb to reach the sunlight.

The term "red" as applied to this strong giant is more apt than color words often are in the case of other trees. Its fitness is most clearly demonstrated by the leaves, which are deep red when they unfold in early spring and a dark, rich maroon in autumn. There is often a red tinge in the leaf stems, too, while the inner bark has a ruddy hue and the young twigs are almost terra cotta. I have never seen a suggestion of red, on the other hand, in the wood or in the normally dark, gray-brown old bark.

This is probably the commonest Oak in the rolling, good-soil woodlands of the eastern states north of New York. Leaves alone are a doubtful means of identification, for those of most Oaks vary their form somewhat even on the same tree, and at a quick glance the Red's foliage is much like that of the Pin, Scarlet, and Black species. It can never be confused, of course, with the rounded-lobe leafage of the White, Post, Bur, and Basket Oaks, or the relatively

narrow, small-lobed patterns of the Chestnut and Chinquapin forms. Perhaps your best plan, as far as field identification is concerned, is to look for leaves with sharp 1- to 3-pointed lobes and only moderate indentation, and then scratch around on the ground underneath the tree to see if you can find at least the remains of a good-sized, fattish, and definitely shallow-cupped acorn that will pretty much clinch the case. Incidentally, the size, shape, and cup proportions of any acorn are quite reliable guides to the identity of the tree which produced it, and collecting the various kinds seen on the ground during an early autumn tramp through Oak-inhabited woods can easily prove an absorbing as well as an instructive pastime. There is as much exterior contrast between a Red Oak's stout, heavy acorn and a slim one from a White Oak as there is between a middle-European peasant and a native New England farmer.

I suspect there is at least a hint in all these comments that the Red Oak's best use is as a woodland tree, or perhaps for rather distant background planting on large home grounds where its great size and rather uncompromising form will not be too dominating. On occasion, though, it can be splendidly effective on those building sites of moderate size which have been reclaimed from heavy woods and are purposely left sprinkled with enough big trees to keep the ground quite fully shaded in summer. Here its high branching habit, lofty crown, and long-lived ruggedness are important assets, for they mean plenty of woodsy shelter while still permitting good views, air circulation, and abundant clean ground for rhododendron, daffodil, and other appropriate plantings beneath them.

In this connection it is well to remember that at least the upper foot of soil beneath large, established oaks of any of the deciduous species is quite certain to be acid, a natural condition which may well arise from the tannic-acid content of the tree as a whole and its transmission to the soil through the falling and rotting away of the old leaves. Consequently, preferable plants for underplanting should be at least acid-tolerant. Besides the rhododendrons and daffodils already mentioned, the list could include mountain-laurel, leucothoë, pieris, most trilliums, and all of the azaleas. One of the most delightful daffodil plantings I know is on a piece of rocky, rolling land fully shaded in summer by large White and Red Oaks beneath which hundreds of narcissus have been naturalized to complete an unforgettable picture.

SASSAFRAS

If you were to set out deliberately to invent a tree with a maximum number of oddities, you would need an excellent imagination to outdo the Sassafras (*Sassafras variifolium*), one of the frequent native species in the region from Maine to Florida and westward into Michigan, Kansas, Oklahoma, and Texas. To a few

disdainful souls it may rate no better than a weed tree, but many more esteem it highly for its picturesque form, its orginalities, and, above all else, its varying beauties throughout the year.

The Sassafras genus is a very small one—a single American member, another in Asia, and a third on the island of Formosa. Our representative grows in a wide variety of soils, though it seems to have a definite preference for locations that are thoroughly drained. When well satisfied, it may ultimately reach a height of 50 or more feet and 3-foot trunk diameter, but most of us know it as a rather slender 20- or 30-footer with smallish, wiggly branches which, quite horizontal in general direction, usually manage to turn upward at the tips.

Apart from its structure, the special interests of the Sassafras begin quite early in the spring, when the buds which tip each greenish twig start to swell and quite suddenly the tree is transformed by hundreds of pale greeny-yellow candelabra as the blossom clusters and the young leaf points step out into the sunshine. A few days of this, and then the yellow tone changes to a soft red tinge that suffuses many of the expanding velvety leaves.

It is at this mid-spring stage that country folk pause to pluck and munch a handful of the aromatic, mitten-shaped new leaves, unexpectedly tender and with a refreshing flavor as distinctive as any I know in all nature. Later, when they are more mature, both texture and taste are tough and crude; but then who would want to eat them anyway, with so many wild strawberries glowing in the June meadows?

Nor does the interest of the leaves end here, for on each tree you will find three kinds—one shaped like a regular single-thumb mitten, another with two "thumbs," and the third with no thumb. They all turn pleasantly yellow in the fall, though not as brightly as the pungent-tasting roots. As a size gauge, the leaves and the fruits are shown here on a background of 1-inch squares.

In late summer, when its little red-stemmed, dark blue fruits ripen, the Sassafras becomes a mecca for the robins, vireos, and other local birds which seem to find in them a welcome change of diet. Why I never sampled them myself, I don't quite know; perhaps it's because they usually are too high in the air to be readily accessible from the ground.

In babyhood the bark of the Sassafras is yellow-green, a tone which persists in the small twigs throughout the tree's life. Before long, though, the texture of the trunk bark roughens into light brown squarish blocks tinged with buff in the crevices. These persist until you begin to accept them as the final phase, and then a third stage begins as the pattern roughens still more and settles into more or less vertical yet weaving ridges like long waves flowing up and down the trunk.

Inside the bark you find a dull orange wood that is soft, light, and coarse-grained, with, of course, a tinge of that distinctive scent which permeates the entire tree. Its chief use is in boxmaking, cooperage, and boatbuilding; for other purposes it is too weak and brittle. Rather more positive is the aromatic oil that is distilled from the bark, twigs, and roots.

Transplanting even a young Sassafras from the wild is no easy matter, for its taproot strikes deep, and unless you excavate it practically intact, the survival of the tree will be a matter of touch and go. Your best chance will be with a really young seedling—no taller than 2 feet, if you can find one that small. Autumn is likely to be the most favorable season for trying the experiment. Fortunately, a few nurseries grow Sassafras for sale, and from them you can purchase at reasonable prices 8- or 10-foot trees much better equipped to stand the shock of moving than those collected from your neighboring field or woodland.

From my observation, few insect pests bother this tree. Its chief flying enemy seems to be the Japanese beetle, which disfigures the foliage rather badly in occasional years, though apparently this has no serious effect on the victim's health. Also, its leaves, like those of the Wild Cherry, are favorite shrouds for the overwintering cocoons of some of the night-flying moths.

In Indian days, so the story goes, the Onondagas of New York State called the Sassafras Wah-eh-nak-kas, or Smelling Stick. I strongly suspect, too, that they put its roots to some medicinal or beverage use, as they did so many of nature's products. Certainly the white men saw the opportunities in this direction, as witness the sassafras tea and root beer of back-country homes and cross-roads stores long, long before the Era of Wonderful Nonsense was even a haze on the horizon of the future.

WHITE PINE

To my perhaps prejudiced way of thinking, the White Pine (*Pinus strobus*) is the finest member of its race, at least as far as the American species are concerned. It has grace, beauty of color and form, majesty, and outstanding usefulness to mankind. Years ago it was the outstanding source of fine lumber in our northern tier of states—so outstanding that, in our characteristically prodigal American way, we decimated its millions so recklessly and with so little attention to reforesting that today one may look long for a single mature and perfect specimen where once there were thousands.

Normally the White Pine is single-trunked and straight, reaching a height of 75 to 90 feet and sometimes much more. That was what we had in mind to illustrate these pages, but locating such a one out in the open where it could be photographed successfully was such a task that eventually we had to compromise on the one pictured here, which must have suffered some injury in its youth which forced it into such an unethical trunk form. Fully demonstrated, though, is the characteristic shelf-tier formation of the branches which is one of the tree's most notable features as it comes toward old age.

From 1-foot babyhood to 100-foot old age, the White Pine will delight every lover of fine textures with needles of remarkable beauty. One never tires of feeling their almost silky surfaces, the softness of their flexibility, and studying the delicacy of their form and the subtle blue-green color which almost invariably marks them above those of all the other Pines. Always they grow in neat little bundles of five, and in length they will range between 3 and 4 inches long. Individually they are one of Nature's great masterpieces of design and structure; in the mass they have few equals in plumy beauty.

Light, somewhat sandy soil that is well drained is the favorite foothold of the White Pine, and its natural range runs across the country from Newfoundland to Michigan, Illinois, Iowa, and even

Manitoba, southward near the Atlantic coast into New Jersey, and down through the Alleghenies as far as Georgia. Anywhere you meet it you'll recognize it by the characteristics already mentioned and also by the smoothness of the sometimes green-tinged gray bark even on trees of considerable size. I know of no other Pine so sleek in its trunk surface or so supple and graceful in the character of its smaller branches.

White Pines are among the finest of evergreens for ornamental planting, except perhaps in those regions where the blister-rust disease sometimes causes serious disfiguration of the branch tips. They grow rapidly—seedlings have been known to reach a height of more than 50 feet in thirty years—and accept severe pruning better probably than any other tree of their general type. This last characteristic fits them admirably for use as tall hedges and wind-breaks, though personally I wouldn't want to cramp their normal form by making them abide by any such artificial pattern.

Perhaps the White Pine's greatest handicap is its susceptibility to borer attack, especially while quite young. Two insects are the culprits—the white-pine weevil and the white-pine-shoot moth. The grubs of the former girdle the bark of the leader shoot, killing it above the point of injury; those of the latter bore into the lateral shoots in early summer, causing wilting of the tips. In both cases full control is difficult. The standard procedure is prompt cutting off and burning of the affected parts *below* the point where the pests are at work.

In view of the extent to which this grand tree has been exploited by commercial lumber interests, it is fortunate indeed that it grows so readily from seed and can be transplanted with such confidence of success. Someday, perhaps, we will re-create in some degree the superb White Pine forests which our ancestors knew—and thought-lessly destroyed. Indeed, a number of the State Forestry Depart-ments are now definitely encouraging the large-scale planting of this species on suitable vacant lands and saying little about the unsatis-factory Scotch Pine which some of them pushed so vigorously twenty years or so ago. When any country can boast a native tree as splendid as the White Pine, it seems no less than common sense to give it every opportunity to regain at least a semblance of the widespread leadership it once enjoyed.

WHITE
OAK

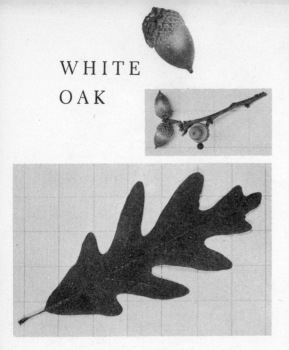

If some able researcher were to conduct a sort of tree lovers' public-opinion poll, the chances are excellent that he'd come up with data indicating that the White Oak (*Quercus alba*) is very close to top scorer in the enthusiasm, if not in the total number, of its admirers. Throughout its natural range it is a prime favorite of native tree connoisseurs from farm boy to Ph.D. Locally famous specimens in countless regions acquire almost the stature of shrines; not even the Elm, popular though it is, inspires quite the same feeling of quiet pride.

The moment you get a good view of a really fine White Oak you understand the reasons for its unfailing appeal. Like most of its tribe, it is impressively tall—anywhere from 50 to well over 100 feet—but that is secondary when compared with the perfect proportions of its short, sturdy trunk and massive, far-reaching, often nearly horizontal branches. From ground line to the highest twig in its broad, rounded crown it is as perfect a demonstration of strength with beauty as you are likely to find in the whole tree world. Even the whitish-gray bark with its perpendicular furrows and ridges is

firm, cleanly designed, and in excellent taste, while the rather glossy edible acorns and large, symmetrically indented leaves are finishing touches which could not be improved.

White Oaks are partial to dryish, gravelly, or sandy hills and flatlands from Maine through lower Quebec and Ontario to Minnesota and southward from most of this line to northern Florida and Texas. They reach their finest development, perhaps, in the Allegheny Mountains and the Ohio River valley, where trees with a trunk diameter of about 7 feet are sometimes encountered. The White Oak is, of course, a most valuable timber tree, and its hard, close-grained wood is put to a variety of uses, including agricultural implements, shipbuilding, interior house finish, baskets, and various kinds of construction.

For landscape planting this is probably the finest of all the Oaks, assuming merely that the surroundings are spacious enough for it to develop the commanding presence of which it is capable. In addition to the year-round and always satisfying beauty of its frame and outline, its large leaves (to 8 inches long) are deep olive green, lustrous, and turn to a somewhat subdued wine red in autumn. It makes a better specimen shade tree than any other one of its family, with the possible exception of the evergreen Live Oak of the South, because of its symmetry of outline and the large circle of the branches. Indeed, to plant it in among other trees would be a waste of golden opportunity, for a typical White Oak even partially concealed by other growths misses much of its effectiveness. Finally, if you should happen to fancy the idea, two of its massive lower branches will make perfect anchorages for a hammock, for they'd never let you down—no, not in a hundred years, or two hundred. If this seems a flippant suggestion, please forgive it on the score that it is being written in the midst of a sweltering New York afternoon.

As has been mentioned elsewhere on these pages, Oaks are rather deep-rooting trees and for this as well as other practical reasons should be secured from good nurseries which grow them in such a way that they develop more compact root systems than wild trees and therefore transplant better. They are all such long-lived, thoroughly satisfactory trees that the cost of a top-quality nursery specimen is a fully justified investment.

BLACK
LOCUST

The inclusion of the Black Locust (*Robinia pseudoacacia*) in this volume came only after considerable soul searching and discussion. You see, while this hundred-per-cent American is a prime favorite of thousands who like it for its unique appearance, its indifference to drought and cold, its feathery leafage and the intense fragrance of its white pea-shaped blossoms, there are other thousands who scorn it as a pest tree forever coming up from seeds and suckers where it isn't wanted, as a sufferer from disfiguration by borers in some localities, and as a bearer of brutally large, sharp thorns along its branches and young trunk. I personally belong to both camps, illogical though that position may sound, and so must throw the case upon the mercy of the court!

Few species of trees are of such widely varying appearance at different seasons of the year as this original native of the Southeast and Midwest which is now, through cultivation, found in almost all parts of the United States east of the Rockies. It is one of our latest trees to leaf out in the spring, but when it does start, its outer branch portions are quickly clothed in the airiest of light green foliage that ripples and billows so easily in the breeze that at a little distance it reminds one of some filmy, shifting veil. Not until June would you suspect it of even planning to blossom; then, suddenly, pale patches appear near the top of the tree, and in a few days the whole contour is overlaid with white sprays from which a rich, heavy fragrance spreads afar and draws a million bees.

For many generations this odd tree has been highly valued for the durability of its greenish-yellow wood, especially when, as posts and supports of various kinds, it is in direct contact with the soil.

Strangely enough, when freshly cut, it is rather soft, but after seasoning it becomes exceedingly hard and resistant to the effects of exposure. Country folk often prize it even more than Red-cedar as fence-post material, particularly after its bark has been removed.

Locust is normally a fairly straight-trunked tree with, at maturity, relatively short and "wiggly" branches that grow out more or less horizontally. It may reach a height of 70 or 80 feet and a butt diameter of 3 or 4, and commonly it is found in groups or groves rather than as isolated specimens. It is a rapid grower which, as it gains stature, tends to lose its lower branches until eventually it has the rugged, picturesque appearance so well portrayed in the accompanying winter photograph. The trunk bark of an old one is sepia brown and notably rough, but on the slender new twigs which even a fully mature tree produces freely the bark color is a pleasant ruddy tan. I know of no other tree which, when bare of leaves, looks so primitive against a winter sky.

66

It has always seemed to me that the Locust was never put together quite right—a characteristic which, in a way, gives it a special, if somewhat uncomplimentary, interest. It looks as if it had been assembled from parts of several other trees, all widely different from each other. There is no apparent harmony between the stubby limbs of an old-timer and the delicacy of the twigs, leaves, and blossoms which terminate them. Though its wood is designed for long service, borers can riddle it with ease and evident enthusiasm. Insect attack may wreck its figure before it really grows up, but its roots will continue sending up strong shoots for years. Heavy curved thorns of formidable strength armor it against man, beast, or serpent, yet it bears no edible fruit or other asset that might need protection. It is at once somber and gay, gaunt and delicate, tough and fragile, forbidding and inviting. In a word, a complete individualist, intriguing in its very inconsistencies.

Black Locust is not a tree for home-grounds planting, for its susceptibility to the borers which have already been mentioned and to a very minute leaf-eating pest which apparently is extending its range is too great a liability to pile on top of the tree's incurable invasiveness. I understand that these insect pests—particularly the borers—do little if any damage to those Locusts which have been introduced into Europe, so over there the species has won considerable prominence as an ornamental. But with us perhaps the wisest course is just to enjoy it where it happens to be, often growing wild or nearly so and sometimes towering high above some old estate to whose venerable air it provides the crowning touch.

BLACK SPRUCE

Botanically speaking, the Black Spruce (*Picea mariana*) is only one member of a tree genus made up of some thirty-eight species found in various parts of the world. Practically, though, when you see a fine specimen of it you are likely to forget that there are any other kinds, so fully satisfying is the one before you. For the Black Spruce in its typical form is a slender, well-porportioned spire, many-branched and clothed in stiff, dark bluish-green needles dusted with a whitish bloom. For perhaps two thirds of its height the limbs droop markedly, then seem to change their minds and curve upward at the tips; in the upper third of the tree they become horizontal, then grow more and more upward as they approach the slightly rounded tip.

This, as I say, is the typical form and the one you are most likely to encounter in heights of anywhere from 20 to 90 feet or so—the lower trees in the North, the taller in the southern mountains. The Black Spruce, though, grows over such a vast territory, both in area and altitude, that it is subject to a great range of variations. Actually it is found from Labrador and Nova Scotia clear across the continent to the Yukon and Mackenzie rivers, and southward irregularly as far as the Great Smokies in Tennessee. I have been especially interested in its habits in New Hampshire's Presidential Range where, on the lower slopes, it grows in normal proportions but becomes increasingly smaller as you ascend until, above timber line, it is hardly more than a gnarled, rugged mat hugging the ground wherever jumbled boulders give it some protection from the sweeping wind. You can walk on the tops as if you were on a spring mattress until a weak spot is encountered and you break through with disconcerting suddenness to the ground a foot or two below.

Out of all these characteristics arises the fairly obvious conclusion that the home-grounds potentialities of the Black Spruce are pretty much restricted to the northern tier of states—and Canada, of course. In the upper part of this area, where it remains relatively small, it can be used effectively for windbreaks, for small groups, or as a single specimen where a strong, rather slender accent is needed, even on fairly small properties. In the more southern part of its range, though, its greater stature virtually limits it to large places. In any case, it is well to remember that the Black Spruce is a rather somber tree and so should be used with more than usual discretion. Personally, I like it best in its native haunts and settings, to which it is so perfectly suited. But maybe that's just a notion.

From a worldly standpoint the Black Spruce is a tree of considerable importance. Its light yellowish wood is not strong, as woods go, but enormous quantities of it are converted into paper pulp and the construction industry uses it widely in the form of lumber. It is one of the big contributors to the world's supply of commercial spruce gum, and spruce beer, that grand old beverage of the backwoods, is evolved from the fresh twigs of this tree and the quite similar Red Spruce.

70

WHITE
ASH

The story of the White Ash (*Fraxinus americana*), like that of the Oaks, Maples, and Hickories, is bound closely with the record of early colonial days and the men who quite literally hewed their homes out of what was then the American wilderness. Not that the tree appealed especially to any sentimental or esthetic impulse in those resourceful pioneers, for in point of fact it is no more impressive or commanding than a dozen other kinds that the settlers took more or less in their stride. What really won for it their high esteem was its downright usefulness in surmounting their practical problems of building and heating, clearing the land, breaking ground for crops, and countless smaller matters that the days brought forth. For the strong, clean-grained, enduring wood of the White Ash served many practical ends and even today vies with that of the Oak for the honor of being the most valuable, commercially, produced by any American timber tree.

The White Ash grows into a big, straight, heavy-limbed tree which may ultimately reach a height of more than 100 feet and a butt diameter of 5 feet. In open country it tends to be rather broad and rounded, but in the forest it is tall and much straighter. These general characteristics seem to hold throughout its whole range from Nova Scotia to Minnesota, Kansas, Texas, and Florida, and so does its adaptability to varying soils and situations.

Superficially, you can tell a White Ash by several obvious characteristics. One is the gray-brown quite conservatively ridged and furrowed bark of the trunk, and another is the stubby, stout look and brittleness of the small twigs in their smooth, often greenish-gray overcoats. From late spring until fall its leaves, too, distinguish it clearly from all other trees except a few species of its own genus, for they are compound, around 12 inches long, and divided into three or four matched pairs of leaflets with another single leaflet

at the very tip; they are a rather dull light green on top, silvery beneath, and turn yellow in the fall. Finally, the greenish, catkin-like late spring flowers (staminate on one tree, pistillate on another) are followed by great clusters of slender, oar-like winged fruits that spin gaily away from the female trees when the right autumn gale comes roaring past.

White Ashes grow fast, for all their ruggedness of wood and structure, and have been known to reach a height of nearly 50 feet

in thirty years. They prefer rich, well-drained soil, as most potentially big trees do, and are virtually bug and disease-free except for occasional attacks by the common lilac borer in some localities. When this pest does happen to put in an appearance, its presence may be indicated by large scars on the trunk and by holes from which sawdust-like material protrudes, sometimes on the smaller branches, which may snap off at the point of injury. Control is not easy if the infestation is a serious one, but in an average case the beasts can be handled by squeezing nicotine paste (made for the purpose) into the individual holes.

In view of the myriad seeds a fair-sized White Ash produces every year, and the distance they are often carried by a strong wind, it might be expected that the tree could be rather a nuisance on the home grounds by scattering offspring in all kinds of inappropriate places. Perhaps I have merely been lucky, but I have never been bothered by such developments despite personal experience with several different properties where this wholesale seed scattering was

an annual event. Or it may be that the viability (ability to sprout) of the seeds is low, or that many of them are blown loose from the tree before they are really ripe. Montague Free, however, reports that the White Ash is the "weed" tree on his place at Hyde Park, New York, so evidently its seeds are not always so considerate.

Young White Ash trees are offered by many nurseries in the northern states, and they offer no particular problems in either planting or subsequent care. Let me make two suggestions, though, in case you decide to plant one or more: first, that you make sure the location provides ample space for the future development of this really substantial tree; and second, that it looks much more at home in informal, country-like surroundings than it does on neatly tailored properties.

SHAGBARK
HICKORY

To say that the Shagbark (*Carya ovata*) is esthetically beautiful would be a distortion of facts; actually its form and textures often verge closely on the grotesque. But to deny it a high, if not the highest, place among the best-loved trees of America would be to flout one of this country's dearest traditions, too often forgotten in the turmoil of these changing days.

For in the horse-and-buggy era the Shagbark was part and parcel of the farmlands, as integral with rural living as the smell of new-plowed land, the heat of hayfields, the cows waiting at the barway toward the close of day. To the working of the soil it contributed tough, enduring hoe handles for the men and whiffletrees for the farm wagons; to the indoor hours, bushels of sweet-kerneled nuts and cords of perfect firewood, vital with heat and all but sparkless. In the smokehouse it was the prime fuel for the curing of meats. Its broad, leathery leaves barred the sun from the spring water in the harvesters' drinking bucket. Every farm boy, every squirrel, every sentinel crow in the white days of winter knew it as a friendly provider of good things and honored it for their provision.

All this the Shagbark was in earlier days, and much of its honor

still lingers in the back country despite the inroads of the automotive age. I never see a rugged, ragged old giant of the race dominating a hillside pasture without its seeming a sort of monument to American traits that must never pass.

The natural range of this most noteworthy Hickory runs roughly from lower Maine, Michigan, and Minnesota southward to Florida, Alabama, Mississippi, and Texas. Rich uplands are its favorite location, and there it sometimes reaches a butt diameter of 3 or 4 feet and a height of perhaps 100. As a youngster of good-sized sapling age its bark is dark gray and smooth, but with more maturity comes an increasing roughness on the trunk and larger branches, followed by the peculiar loosening into partially detached strips which give the tree its name. From that stage the bark color gradually lightens to a pale brownish gray, a wholly lovely tone in the hazy autumn scene and under the full glare of a winter sun.

For all its rugged individualism, every grown-up Shagbark has its interlude of delicate springtime beauty. About the time the Red Maple flowers appear the terminal buds on the Hickory begin to swell until, within their green-buff envelopes, one feels that a great

77

blossom at least as large as a Magnolia's must be forming. But instead there emerge at last the palest of pale green compound leaves and, often, trios of pendent green catkins carrying the pollen for the female flowers. For a week or more these vital parts of Shagbark life retain their delicacy of tone and texture before, with full development, the catkins fulfill their duty and fall to the ground and the far larger leaflets begin to acquire the coarser surfaces of maturity. Not until midsummer are you likely to notice, at the very tips of the twigs, the little green globes within whose thick walls the sweet, almost white nuts of October are growing. But the gray squirrels know what's coming, and long before the husks begin to split they will start to comb the tree in unbelievable acrobatics and the ground beneath will be spattered with the chips discarded from their gnawing.

Shagbarks are attacked on occasion by a variety of insect pests, including borers, aphids, and leaf-eating caterpillars of startling size and appearance (the hickory horned devil, larva of the regal moth). However, these enemies as a rule do no serious damage, and if the tree is in normally good condition they can be largely disregarded.

Much as I dislike to admit it, as an ornamental tree this member of the Hickory tribe leaves something to be desired, especially on grounds marked by a degree of sophistication. There is that about its character which calls for country spaciousness and informality, and introducing it among the limitations of suburbia seems almost on a par with keeping a bird dog in the city.

If, though, you have plenty of space and good, well-drained soil where one or more of these trees can develop without appreciable competition with other growths, by all means give the Shagbark favorable thought. It is difficult to move when of any real size, but seedling trees 3 or 4 feet tall are available from some nurseries and should present no difficulties. Lest this small size lead to gloomy speculations as to your own age before the tree is big enough to amount to much, take courage from the fact that Shagbarks, especially in their earlier years, are fairly rapid growers. And remember, too, the story of the farmer whose son and grandson, successively, refused to start a Walnut grove because it would take too long to produce a crop, only to see the old man finally plant the nuts himself and live out his final days in affluence sprung from his faith in the processes of time and nature!

HEMLOCK

I shall always count it a privilege to have been raised in Hemlock country. Every phase of this grand evergreen, from inch-high seedling to hundred-foot giant, was as familiar to us country youngsters as our own dooryards. In spring we climbed to the owls' and crows' nests high in the trees' dense upper crowns; in summer we sprawled contentedly in the scented coolness beneath the tent-like branches; in winter we fell silent as we entered the mystery of the snow-laden "big green woods." Whether our fishing, berrying, or chestnutting expeditions took us to sunny meadows, dry hill fields, or hardwood ridges, we generally managed to include at least a bit of Hemlock woods because of the vague, compelling spell, never defined but always sensed, which came upon us only there.

Dismissing such almost prenatal influence, though, the Hemlock (*Tsuga canadensis*) is at least as "best-loved" as the American Elm, the Tulip-tree, the Shagbark, or any other favorite one can name. Though its natural range is pretty much limited to Delaware on the south (except in the mountains), the Mississippi on the west, the Canadian border on the north, and the Atlantic on the east, its feathery grace, its size, and above all the clean, alert green of its year-round "needles" have carried its fame to the far corners of the land. Straight of trunk, long of branch, majestic in maturity but surprisingly versatile in its adaptability to landscaping uses, it is perhaps the most satisfying all-rounder among our native evergreen trees. Many a smallish garden has its Hemlock hedge, restrained for years to a height of 8 feet or so by means of regular topping and impenetrably dense as a result of careful shearing. There is no finer tree to plant as a tall background along a boundary line or to group in a far corner where a dominant accent of year-

round effectiveness is needed. Where space is available, a Hemlock grove of outstanding charm can be created in surprisingly few years, for the tree grows rapidly in reasonably good soil and thrives on the companionship of its own kind. Finally, a single specimen in the right spot may well become the star tree of the whole place, for its beauty grows with the years, and its years are many.

In all fairness, it must be admitted that Hemlocks do have trouble, sometimes. They don't really like very windy positions, though several experiences with toughening up trees under cultivation, as well as long observation of their reactions in the wild, leads me to feel that their sensitivity in this respect is far less serious than some people would have us believe. There is no doubt, unfortunately, that they are sometimes so badly plagued by red spider mites in hot summer weather that the normal healthy green of their foliage turns grayish and unhappy—a situation which can lead to serious weakening of the tree unless it is sprayed in the early stages with one of the standard "summer" oils or with a solution made by dissolving one pound of glue in warm water and diluting with enough more water to make up eight gallons of liquid.

In regions where the Hemlock grows freely in the wild it is usually possible to locate a virtually unlimited supply of young natural seedlings and collect as many as you may want. This is a slow way of getting real results, of course, but if you are the patient type it is something to think about. Seedlings up to 18 inches tall are usually easy to transplant in early spring and, given room and some annual pruning, will generally develop into good, well-shaped specimens. The alternative to such a product is to buy first-class nursery-grown plants, preferably in early spring. Whatever their source, be sure to keep the new trees thoroughly watered until they are well rooted and really start to grow.

Besides the particular species we have been talking about there are several other kinds found in different parts of the country. Best known, perhaps, are the Carolina Hemlock of our southern mountains and the Western Hemlock on the Pacific coast. Both are splendid trees with the general characteristics of *Tsuga canadensis* and susceptible to the same sort of uses and treatment. In fact, the whole Hemlock genus might be described truthfully in just one word: "excellent."

TULIP-TREE

The United States is fortunate in the number and variety of its large trees, but within the area where it naturally grows you would look far to find one more impressive, more truly majestic than the Tulip-tree (*Liriodendron tulipifera*) at its best. From central New England to Wisconsin, and southward as far as Florida and Alabama, it is the outstanding feature of many a landscape from year's end to year's end.

Its form is variable, but often its frame of limbs is built around a single, mast-straight trunk which, under favorable conditions, may attain a diameter of 8 feet and a height of nearly 200. In other lower specimens the trunk sometimes forks at mid-height, and trees with two or even three trunks are not uncommon. But whatever the structural variations, always there are the broad bright green leaves, the tulip shaped yellow-green and orange blossoms, the gold and russet pile against the sky when autumn transforms the countryside with color. Other trees may be more graceful or rugged, dense or fantastically gaunt, but the Tulip is always the well-balanced, upstanding American, a leader in any company.

83

Tulip-trees are rapid, vigorous growers and often reach their greatest height in woodlands, where this characteristic helps them to outstrip most other species in the unending race to win and retain a place in the sun. Under such conditions the column-like trunk of a big one may not show a single limb in the first fifty feet or more—one of the most compelling sights I know in our eastern forests. If you could examine the twigs far above, you'd find them a glossy, somewhat reddish chestnut brown—an appropriate combination with the firm-patterned character of the brownish-gray bark on the bole and larger branches.

It is surprising that so few people are familiar with the blossoms which give the tree its most common name. True, they are not gaudy, and when seen from below (the usual position) are nearly hidden by the surrounding leaves. But, after all, they do grow at the twig tips, frequently on fairly low branches, and the spread of their petals is as much as 3 or 4 inches. The time to look for them is late May or early June, and if you like soft, sun-warmed colors you'll find the discovery of even one abundantly worth while.

It is from these flowers, of course, that the pointed, cone-like seed heads develop, pale straw-colored when ripe and standing up against the early winter sky like wee, pale candle flames until some roaring gale scatters their winged contents far and wide. And from those wind-borne myriads, spinning into the flower border, lodging under the shrubs, forever snatching an opportunity to make actual contact with the soil from which their parent sprang, countless seedlings will pop up to create an opportunity and a nuisance too —the first because they are easily transplanted to desired spots while not over a foot or so in height, and the second because they can constitute a real weeding problem. I once moved such a seedling to rich soil at the edge of a sunny field, and within ten years it was twenty feet tall and gaining stature at an annual rate of more than a yard. But Tulip-trees of any appreciable size are tough customers to transplant, due to the deep-striking character of their roots.

Tulips are naturally healthy, trouble-free fellows, though it must be admitted that sometimes their twigs are attacked by a large, soft-scale insect and their leaves by a green aphis whose excretion of honeydew leads to the development of a sooty fungus which

badly disfigures them. The scale, however, can be controlled by a
dormant oil-emulsion spray in spring, and a nicotine-sulphate spray
will take care of the aphids if they appear. Personally, I know far
more Tulip-trees without either of these pests than with them, so
perhaps you don't need to worry much if you decide that you'd

like to own one of these superb trees and have a place large enough to accommodate it even when it grows to full size.

Some kinds of trees have numerous common names, but to my knowledge this species has only four—Tulip-tree, Tulip Poplar, Whitewood, and Yellow Poplar. The third of these is obviously a reference to the color of its straight-grained inner wood. Despite its comparative softness, this wood is unlikely to split or warp and, since it is easily worked, has many uses for cabinetmaking, woodenware, interior house trim, etc. North Carolina alone has produced vast quantities of Whitewood lumber, for the tree grows well there.

PIN OAK

It is perhaps a sort of heritage from our Anglo-Saxon forebears that leads us to think of the Oak as a symbol of rugged strength. Certainly the ancient Oaks of England are gnarled and massive enough to justify such a symbolism, and most of our American species also bear out the idea when they approach the age of true maturity. The one outstanding exception, in those areas where it is native, is the Pin Oak (*Quercus palustris*). Even when it has carried out the family tradition of reaching a ripe but notably strong old age, it displays far too many comparatively slender branches to suggest much in the way of ruggedness.

I confess a rather special partiality to the Pin Oak. It is such an individualist, so determined to go its own way and mold its own character regardless of certain important racial tendencies. Whereas the leaves of most Oaks are coarse-textured and somewhat heavy-handed in size and outline, the Pin Oak's are definitely on the graceful, finely chiseled side, smooth and rather glossy on the surface and with their edges clearly cut into deep indentations and sharp-pointed lobes. The bright, deep olive green of their upper surface has a clean-washed look, and there is nothing muddy or indefinite about the rich cardinal-red color which comes to them in autumn. Even the acorns—cute little fat fellows usually less than ½ inch long and nestled in tight-scaled cups or caps—have a pleasantly refined look.

Pin Oaks are moist-ground trees by preference, though perfectly amenable to average conditions. Their natural range extends from central Massachusetts westward to southeastern Missouri, Kansas, northern Arkansas, eastern Oklahoma and central Kentucky, and southward into Virginia. They're tall fellows, sometimes reaching a height of 80 feet, and, in the Ohio River bottom lands, well over 100 feet. Sometimes you see them growing in actual swamps, apparently unworried about their constantly wet feet.

Structurally, you could never mistake one of them for any other Oak. I have already mentioned the large number and comparative slenderness of the branches, but this is only part of the story. Equally characteristic is the horizontal branch growth of many of them, a habit which tends to develop into downright drooping, especially in the lower half of trees of some age. Along with this goes a sometimes astonishing twigginess—many hundreds of

branchlets so small that they may be the origin of the "pin" part of the tree's name. Only when very old does a Pin Oak tend to lose its characteristic symmetry of outline. All these characteristics, plus the dark brownish gray of its trunk bark, make it one of the easily identified members of the Oak tribe.

There is a widespread belief that all Oaks are slow-growing and rather difficult to transplant. Some species may partially justify this reputation, but the Pin is not among them. As a matter of fact, it grows as rapidly as most other desirable shade trees and its fibrous-rooted habit fits it admirably to transplanting, especially when nursery-grown. Another big point in its favor as a home-grounds tree is its comparative freedom from serious insect or disease troubles; occasionally cankerworms or some other epidemic caterpillar will spoil the perfection of its foliage, but that's not too much of a handicap. Transplanting can be done in either fall or early spring (midwinter, too, for really large specimens, if you're ready to pay the price!), and a good practical size in most cases is anywhere from 6 to 12 feet in height. Standard tree-planting practice should be followed—an amply large hole, good soil worked in among the roots and tramped firm, watering and either staking or guying to keep the trunk vertical until the roots have taken a really firm hold.

Quite obviously, since the Pin Oak eventually becomes a really large tree, it needs considerable room and so is not a good selection for many small properties. In deciding for or against it, don't think of the tree in terms of the trim little fellow you see in the nursery, but rather as a bold, symmetrical mass 50 feet or more in height and 30 or 40 feet wide. If you have space enough to accommodate a beauty of that size without throwing your planting scheme out of balance, you can go ahead with full confidence that your new Pin Oak will never let you down.

BLACK
WALNUT

Rugged and all but gaunt in the bare days of winter, a canopy of airy grace and symmetry when the sun sifts through its multitude of summer leaves, the Black Walnut (*Juglans nigra*) is a tree of marked contrasts yet over-all consistency. Though its moods and manners change with the seasons (and quite as radically), it never under any circumstances loses that competent, quiet poise which marks it as one of the great gentlemen among American trees.

It was this strong individualist of the eastern, central, and southern states which furnished the famous Black Walnut wood upon which was built one of our most notable furniture and cabinet-making eras. Deep brown in color, coarse-grained, hard, and aromatic, it can be given a beautiful and very lustrous finish of which one never tires. Before its merits were recognized countless mighty trees were thoughtlessly destroyed in colonial land-clearing operations, and later men felled millions more to fill the demand for commer-

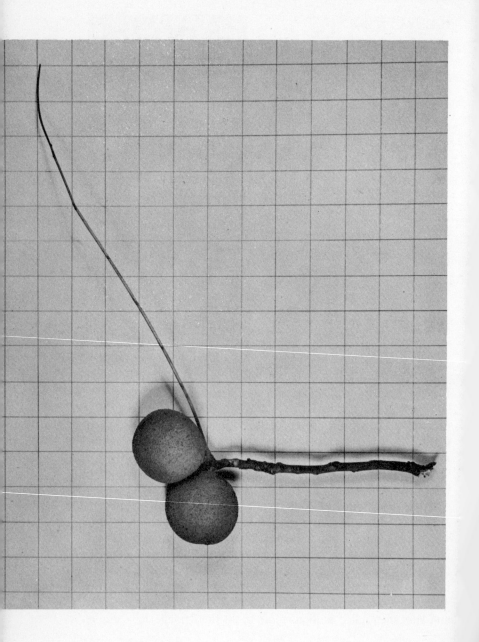

cial uses. The result was that our great Black Walnut population was dangerously depleted, and since one of these trees must be some 80 years old before it is large enough for lumbering, the price commanded by its wood reached fantastic heights. Whether the species ever regains more than a tithe of its one-time abundance is problematical indeed.

The Black Walnut has been known to reach a height of 150 feet, on a straight, massive trunk close to 8 feet in diameter near the butt; but one sees few today that are more than 100 feet tall. Even that is a very sizable tree, especially when it is so symmetrical and roundheaded. Usually the lower branches are horizontal and fairly wide-spreading, while the rest grow upward at sharper and sharper angles as they approach the crown.

The whole effect is wholesome and satisfying, especially when the twigs are furnished with their graceful, frond-like stems of pointed yellow-green leaves that turn to pleasant yellow in the autumn.

The fruits of this tree are perhaps the richest of our native nuts, and particularly famous for the flavor they impart to cakes. Each one, when it falls from the tree, is covered by a thick aromatic and rather pulpy green husk which completely masks the thick, rough-surfaced actual nut with its rather small kernel. This combination makes the Black Walnut a real problem from the food standpoint, for unless the conditions under which its crop is harvested and ripened are exactly right, the oil which invests all parts of the fruit will turn rancid and the kernels will be ruined. No nut lover's disappointment can match that of finding nothing edible after the trouble of cracking open one of these amazingly resistant customers. But certainly, when you do find a good one, all other disappointments are forgotten.

I have been on friendly terms with Black Walnut trees for a good many more years than I care to admit, and count them among my special favorites. Two little notes of warning, though, in all fairness: don't build a house under the branch spread of a Black Walnut, lest your autumn nights be hideous with the crash and rumble of the big, heavy nuts falling on the roof; and don't, as you value your comfort, stroll carelessly beneath such a tree at this same season unless you wear a crash helmet!

PECAN

Three decades or so ago a national poll on the question of our most famous nut-bearing native tree probably would have been won by the American Chestnut. But much water has flowed over the dam since those years, and disease has all but wiped out the Chestnut from the vast area it once dominated. Today it is the Pecan (*Carya pecan*), largest of the Hickory clan, that would lead our nut-bearers in any such test, and with excellent reason. More than any other it owes its fame to the excellent food quality of its nuts, an important crop in those areas where they are commercially produced.

Pecans are big, handsome trees that range in height from 70 to 80 feet—even up to 170 feet on occasion, with a 2-yard trunk diameter. Well formed and rather slender, with rough, pale buffish bark that is strongly seamed, they are definitely ornamental as well as useful, though one must admit that, unlike most others of the Hickory genus, the wood is too brittle to have much commercial value. From the Pecans' own point of view, this last characteristic is actually an advantage, at least here in the United States, where ax and saw are so greedily wielded on all species that make good lumber.

By nature the Pecan grows from eastern Iowa south through Missouri, Indiana, and southern Illinois to the western parts of Kentucky and Tennessee, and thence into Arkansas, Alabama, Mississippi, Oklahoma, and central Texas. These original limits have been greatly extended by man, of course, so that nowadays you will find the tree in many other parts of the South and even in California, growing both in commercial orchards and as home-grounds trees. By and large, the best development occurs in the moist, rich soil of bottom lands, but such conditions do not appear to be essential to good, average growth and health.

Simultaneous with the spring coming of the Pecan's bright yellow-green leaflets—from nine to seventeen of them strung along a stem that may be as long as 20 inches—slim, pendent male catkins develop preparatory to supplying pollen for the much smaller female flowers grouped at the twig tips. It is there, at the very ends of the year's new growths, that the famous nuts are formed in clusters that eventually contain from three to ten or eleven individuals, depending on the thoroughness of the pollination, the vigor of the tree, and other variable factors.

The appearance of the smooth tan-brown mature nut is too well known to need description here, but a fact which is seldom realized outside of the Pecan-growing country is that the thickness of the shell varies considerably between individual trees—and so, too, does the flavor of the kernel. This has naturally led to a long process of selection with a view to growing orchard trees whose yield will have the thinnest "paper" shells covering the largest and sweetest kernels. Many of such commercial orchards are now firmly established, and it is from them that the finest quality nuts reach the market.

As a home-grounds tree the Pecan has many assets, assuming that one has space enough for such a big fellow. Its shape immediately commends it as a provider of shade, and the peculiar character of its foliage keeps that shade from being too dense. Actually, it is one of the finest large ornamental trees of the South, normally healthy and long-lived, responding well to the conditions which home grounds can provide. Nor does its suitability end there, for it also ranks high for planting along wide streets and country roads. Rare indeed is the tree which plays so successfully the dual role of satisfying man's aesthetic senses and the nutritional needs of his body.

Every kind of tree has some troubles of its own, and in the case of the Pecan it's a bird which serves as one of its chief annoyances. The fellow in question is the common sapsucker, one of the woodpecker group, and he does just what his name implies, drilling rows of holes into the trunk and larger branches so he can eat the soft inner bark, and returning later to feast on the oozing sap and the small insects attracted by it. The net result, of course, is some drain on the tree's vitality, and in extreme cases this may become serious.

SUGAR MAPLE

When I looked at the accompanying Sugar Maple photographs, I could not help speculating idly on how many—or how few—of the city-bred motorists who pause to buy "Maple Products" along New England's roadsides realize that many of the trees past which they have whizzed so unheedingly all day are the very ones which provide those sugar blocks, jars of creamy spreads, candies, and jugs of fragrant syrup that lift the breakfast wheat cakes from mediocrity to royal rank.

An idle thought, as I said, and yet its implications cut deeper than may casually appear, for the Sugar Maple (*Acer saccharum*) is a tree of marked importance in regions where it abounds. Just as its sap is a valued item in the economic lives of the country folk, so do its autumn foliage splendor and its impressiveness through the rest of the year contribute richly to the beauty and hence the fame of the landscape. Finally, its pale, hard, close-grained wood is highly valued for cabinetwork and the flooring and interior finish of houses. Under abnormal growth conditions the wood grain may be distorted into that distinctive and most pleasing pattern known as curly or bird's-eye maple. Always, though, you can count on two outstanding interior woodwork advantages: subtle variations in color and pattern, and the ability to take and hold a fine finish.

By nature the Sugar Maple is found in lower Canada and the northern tier of states as far west as Wisconsin, and southward through the Alleghenies to Georgia. From long association, though, I think of it first in terms of those parts of central New York which are largely devoted to dairying. They constitute an open, rolling region, threaded by lush little valleys and dotted with wood lots topping the peaceful pasture hills. Across that high, bright grazing land, sprinkled with distant cattle and the dark lines of fence rows, single Sugar Maples stand sentinel guard, as compact and symmetrical and richly green as the toy trees in a Noah's Ark set. In winter the gales sweep through them mercilessly, in summer the long droughts parch the grass until one wonders if a drop of water remains in all the soil, but the Sugar Maples take everything in stride. Rarely does the ruggedness of their life show more visible effect than an occasional shortness of branches on the side exposed to the strongest prevailing winds. In the truest sense they are landmark trees, anchored deep in the enduring hills.

Comparisons are notoriously prone to be unfair, but to my mind the Sugar Maple is a far finer home-grounds shade tree than the ubiquitous Norway Maple or the brittle Silver Maple which is still so widely planted. Its leaves are of moderate size, and the strongly ascending habit of its branches tends to preclude that extreme density of shade which is one of the Norway's faults. It is surprisingly resistant to storm damage, and its autumn colors are unsurpassed—an unbelievable blend of reds, golds, and greens. It is as easy to grow as any other member of its tribe, at least north of the latitude of New York, and it is notably long-lived. A reasonably productive, well-drained soil is its chief cultural requirement, and it is as good a roadside tree as it is a lawn or background specimen. Oddly enough, any given individual bears its winged seeds every third year or so, instead of annually. Other individuals are likely to operate on different schedules, so where there are several trees in a locality the chances are that every year will find at least one of them producing seeds.

Since Sugar Maples sometimes reach a height of 75 feet (even more if growing among other trees) and a trunk diameter of 4 feet,

they obviously call for good-sized properties. Nursery-grown specimens are usually preferred to any transplanted from the wild, as
they will be better formed and more compactly rooted. You are
unlikely to have any transplanting difficulty, especially if the work is
done in autumn, and as growth is reasonably rapid, you won't have
to wait forever for even a small specimen to reach respectable size.
And I assure you that the waiting will be worth while.

The homemade syrup and sugar possibilities of one—or two or
three—of these Maples? Frankly, I'd forget about that, as only
good-sized trees can be "tapped" without injury, and the amount of
sap required is astonishing—something like ten gallons of sap for
one pound of sugar. The boiling-down procedure is tricky, too, and
calls for considerable experience. So, all told, it hardly seems worth
bothering with.

BLACK
OAK

From Maine to Florida, and on westward to Minnesota and Texas, the Black Oak (*Quercus velutina*) is one of the largest and most impressive members of a tree family famed the world over for its grandeur, long life, and close association with the affairs of men. All told, there are upward of two hundred known species of Oaks, most of them distributed through the temperate and colder parts of the northern hemisphere, but some of them native to the mountainous parts of the tropics. All of them have one physical characteristic in common: the little capped nut or acorn which, despite some variations in color, shape, and size, is the tree's normal means of carrying on the race.

Upon occasion, with luck and opportunity especially in their favor, Black Oaks may attain a height of 150 feet and a trunk diameter of perhaps 6, but 80 and 4, respectively, are more likely to be the maximum figures you'll find. The growth is rather rapid, too, and the branches, while amply strong, usually remain lighter in proportion to the trunk than those of some other Oak species. I have never quite understood the "black" part of the name, unless it comes from the dark gray color of the old outer bark, for the inner bark is orange and the wood itself a quite light, ruddy brown. As in most Oaks, this wood is hard, heavy, and coarse-grained, widely used for construction and barrelmaking. Tannin and a yellow dye called quercitron are extracted from the bark. The latter product, I suppose, is the reason why the tree is sometimes called Yellow-bark Oak.

To me the Black Oak is a rather aloof tree, magnificent but with a grave sort of dignity that is a bit discouraging to easy familiarity. I can't imagine its leaves smiling or dancing about the way the Gray Birches and Aspens do when a sunny breeze blows through them. Nor is there anything vivid about their autumn color, as in the case of the Scarlet and Red Oaks; rather are they on the dull red or orange-brown side, as befits a quiet, self-possessed tree whose social position is thoroughly secure.

Judging by the regions where they grow most abundantly in the wild, Black Oaks quite definitely like dry, gravelly upland soils, but they will do perfectly well under more average conditions. Like several others of their tribe, they are normally long-lived, healthy, well-formed trees, sufficiently fast-growing to stand well up in the list of desirable shade trees for home properties large enough to permit their use without dwarfing the house or interfering with other plantings. My own preference happens to favor planting them as backgrounds or near the property lines, rather than as lawn specimens, because of the perfect naturalness of their effect when used in that way; but that is a personal angle not to be taken as more than a suggestion. In any event, a well-grown young tree transplanted from a good nursery is much better than a run-of-the-mill one because of its superior root system and more symmetrical form. Fall, winter, and early spring are satisfactory planting seasons; if there's a choice, it is perhaps in favor of the first two.

One final thought, in case you have the opportunity and inclination for such things: Black Oaks, and indeed most Oak species, can be grown quite easily from acorns sown outdoors as soon as they are ripe in the autumn. No growth will appear above ground until the following spring, but from then on development will be reasonably rapid. You see, it's an actual fact, and no mere adage, that "great Oaks from little acorns grow."

GIANT
SEQUOIA

Here it is, the far-famed Big Tree of California (*Sequoiadendron giganteum*), mightiest and oldest cone-bearing evergreen in the world. Though its maximum height of 300 feet or so is exceeded by the 364-foot record of its first cousin, the Coast Redwood, the Big Tree is the thicker of the two, measuring as much as a full 37 feet in trunk diameter above the root swelling.

Both species belong to the Sequoia tribe, and at a quick glance have a decided resemblance to each other. Closer observation, though, reveals numerous differences, the most obvious of which is the denser over-all foliage effect of the Big Tree despite the fact that its leaves are far smaller and more scale-like than the flat half-inch "needles" of the Coast Redwood. The cones of the present species are somewhat larger, too, and more pointed. Both trees are alike in having red heartwood and a majesty of stature that must be seen firsthand to be realized.

The Big Tree's natural range is limited to the western slopes of the Sierra Nevada, where it grows chiefly in scattered groves at altitudes of 4,500 to 8,000 feet. This is a colder region than the one farther west where the Coast Redwood is found, and as a natural result the Big Tree is clearly the hardier of the two species. Curiously enough, it is resistant to great heat as well as to extreme cold, and is known to have survived without apparent harm a temperature range of 125°—all the way from 25° below zero to 100° above. Introduced specimens of it are living happily today in Virginia, Delaware, Pennsylvania, and even Rhode Island.

As you might expect of any plant with such great size and life span, the Big Tree changes its appearance considerably as it grows up. In comparative youth it bears slender, short branches well distributed along the trunk from top to bottom, all of them curving upward and, toward the top, shortening and finally forming a pointed crown. After the tree passes the 300-year mark, however,

the lower limbs gradually thin out, while the foliage that remains becomes more and more dense, as though to compensate for the loss. Really old specimens are likely to be branchless for a good hundred feet above the ground, and in its upper reaches the limbs show thick and crooked as if struggling with the weight of the masses of drooping foliage. This is the most imposing stage of all, and the one upon which the tree's fame is largely based. Some of these changing growth effects are shown in the accompanying photographs.

No one knows with any certainty how long a Big Tree can live, but probably the estimates of 4,000 to 5,000 years are not too fantastic. There is good basis, too, for the calculation that a lower trunk diameter of 15 feet indicates an age of about 2,500 years, so that a 30-footer must be far, far older.

The Big Tree is more fortunate than its relative, the Coast Redwood, in that most of the groves in its native Sierras are within the protection of the National Parks and therefore safe at this time from commercial lumbering operations. Yet perhaps we will do well not to become too complacent about this security, for serious fires are an ever-present threat, and there is no telling what the future may bring in the way of relaxed park regulations as emergency measures.

Giant Sequoias produce a fair number of viable seeds, and a movement to use some of these to increase the number of Big Trees now in existence is gaining headway. It is now possible to obtain seedlings that have been started and grown as a nursery project and that can be expected to succeed in many parts of the eastern states if given special care. High altitude is not necessary to their welfare, but they must be protected from wind and receive ample watering in summer drought, besides being mulched in early winter to keep the ground from freezing deeply. This last precaution is particularly important for the first two or three years after planting in the permanent site. With such attention, the youngsters can usually withstand temperatures down to 15° above zero, while mature trees can pull through a winter thermometer reading of 25° below.

If you want to experiment in growing your own Big Tree in our mid-eastern states, try getting a pot-grown seedling and coddle it

110

along for a couple of years by bringing it indoors, pot or tub and all, during cold spells, returning it and its container to their lightly shaded outdoor spot when the weather warms. Growth is usually rapid in young trees, and your specimen may have outgrown even a big tub after a couple of such conditioning years. When that happens, get it out of the tub with as little root disturbance as possible and make the permanent outdoor planting.

PERSIMMON

It seems a far cry from the Persimmon (*Diospyros virginiana*), proletarian favorite of our southern states, to the Ebony of tropical Asia and Africa, whose dense black wood is famed the world over for its aristocratic beauty when shaped and polished by skilled craftsmen. Yet both these trees belong to the same genus, and though their heartwood differs in color, it is notably similar in grain, density, and general character.

The Persimmon's chief claim to popularity rests in its big reddish-yellow berries, though none could deny the additional assets of its graceful uprightness and the rich green of its summer foliage. A perpetual controversy over the edibility of these peculiar 1- to 1½-inch fruits rages between northerners and southerners, the former asserting that one bite of a persimmon will pucker up your mouth for life and the latter announcing that it's about the most delectable fruit in the world if you have sense enough to wait until after frost when it is really ripe. Both sides are right, actually, for an unripe Persimmon "plum" is horribly astringent and holds no hint of the sweet, rich juiciness, flavored somewhat like a date, which fills it on the threshold of winter. Whimsically enough, opossums appreciate ripe persimmons just as heartily as people do and often climb high among the branches to feast on them. It is no uncommon occurrence for two or three opossums to spend most of the night feeding in the same tree.

The real stamping ground of this Ebony cousin is in the states south of Pennsylvania and west to southern Ohio, Missouri, Kansas, and Texas. In all except the higher mountainous parts of this great area, you will find it growing in fields and open woods, preferably where the soil is light and sandy. It rarely becomes more than 50 or 60 feet high, with a trunk diameter of perhaps 18 inches. The leaves, leathery and from 2 to 5 inches long, are definitely

handsome in their disposition on the twigs as well as in their own right. There is nothing noteworthy about the rather inconspicuous flowers, except the fact that the two sexes are usually borne on different trees, with the result that many of the trees (males, of course) never bear any fruit.

The fruit itself is odd-looking and variable in shape, its usual form somewhat resembling that of a tomato. It has a large, spreading calyx at the stem end, and contains one or several flat, large seeds near its center. This native southern species is not the one which yields the larger, more showy persimmons sometimes seen in our eastern fruit markets; they come from a Japanese species, *Diospyros kaki*, which has been widely planted in the South. Incidentally, the size of our native Persimmon fruit does not seem to increase when the tree is grown under cultivation. The typical orange color ultimately assumed by the fruit does not necessarily indicate complete ripeness, by the way; it often develops long before the fruit is in fit condition to eat.

As already noted, Persimmon wood has some of the qualities of Ebony. It is heavy, hard, and strong, with very fine grain and deep brown to nearly sepia brown in color. Like true Ebony, it takes an excellent polish, and its density and hardness make it valuable for such specialized commercial items as shoe lasts, mallets, shuttles, and bench screws.

Trees may begin bearing when no more than 6 or 8 feet tall, which greatly simplifies the picking problem. When approaching maturity, however, it is a different story: then the fruit is largely confined to the upper branches, far out of reach from the ground.

It's far from easy to transplant a Persimmon—next to impossible, indeed, if the tree is of any size. The seeds germinate readily, however, so if you want a few trees the surest plan is to start them from seed, transplant while still very small, shift to larger and larger pots until they are a foot or so tall, and then set them out where you want them to grow permanently.

AMERICAN ELM

For many, many generations the American or White Elm (*Ulmus americana*) has been an outstanding feature of the New England countryside and that whole vast region which extends westward beyond Lake Superior to the foothills of the Rockies and south to Texas and Florida. In its best-loved form it is a graceful, vase-shaped tree from 50 to 100 or more feet high and so perfectly proportioned that from butt to farthest drooping twig tip there seems to be no check in the smooth flow of its progressive slenderness. Equally impressive, though in a different way, is another type with heavier branches that tend to grow more horizontally and with odd, rugged angles and elbows which form a superbly sturdy pattern against the winter sky. Between these two extremes are many intermediate forms, including the so-called "feathered" elm—striking examples of the variations that sometimes exist in a single species, apparently depending solely on the whim of the individual.

One of the largest Elms in the United States (still standing, I believe) is at Wethersfield, Connecticut; its trunk measures 28 feet in girth. Another giant, of the rugged type, is the Lafayette Elm at Kennebunk, Maine. This one measures over 17 feet around the trunk, and its branches have a widest spread of 131 feet.

It is a national tragedy that the future of such a splendid and widely distributed tree should be gravely menaced by a disease un-

wittingly imported from foreign lands, but that is the situation which faces the American Elm today. The Dutch elm disease has gained a threatening foothold in the Middle Atlantic States and is gradually extending its devastating effects. At best, control by spraying and inoculation is difficult and eradication even more so. Forestry departments are doing the best they can, but since the cutting down and burning of all infected trees, in wooded areas as well as in more settled surroundings, appears to be the only certain way of stamping out the trouble, the task is obviously staggering. That other grand tree, our native Chestnut, has all but vanished from the American scene due to a blight that came from the Orient. It is worth a hard and universally supported fight to keep a similar fate from overtaking the Elm.

Besides its general appearance, identifying marks of the American Elm include its firm brownish-gray bark, divided into flat-topped ridges by many short, perpendicular furrows; its sharply double-toothed leaves; and the fuzzy-edged winged seeds which, ripening about the end of May, follow the clusters of tiny brownish-yellow flowers so noticeable when spring comes hesitantly northward.

Because of its ultimate size and wide-ranging roots, this Elm is not well adapted to planting on small properties. Nursery-grown specimens are more easily moved than wild ones. Where the elm leaf beetle is common several sprayings a year may be needed to keep the foliage looking well.

In selecting a planting site, remember that only when an Elm has things pretty much to itself will it develop the full beauty of which it is capable. This means that, preferably, it should be set at least 50 feet away from the nearest competing tree—even more, if the latter is already of good size. You can generally count on its main branches developing sufficiently high up to arch over the roof of an average house rather than block up the windows, so that a space of 20 to 30 feet between dwelling and tree may be sufficient, other things being equal.

American Elms are not especially good-looking trees while small (up to about 20 feet). From then on they begin to show signs of their handsome mature form and improve in beauty rather rapidly.

PEPPERIDGE

Pepperidge, Sour Gum, Tupelo, Black Gum—these are well-accepted names for the selfsame tree, yet it seems to me that none of them even faintly reflects any inherent characteristic or way of life. Not that this makes any particular difference, for from the time a Pepperidge is knee-high it is so distinctive that you could not possibly mistake it for any other species. Incidentally, it is probably the only American tree that has a famous food named after it—or after them, for Pepperidge bread originated almost within the branch spread of two enormous specimens as impressive as the patriarch shown here.

The natural range of the Pepperidge (*Nyssa sylvatica*) is from Maine to Florida and west to Texas, Missouri, Michigan, and the lower part of Ontario. Throughout much of this territory it seems to prefer a low, wet location, frequently adjacent to rivers, swamps, and ponds. Often, however, you will find spendid specimens growing under conditions which, at least outwardly, are the exact opposite of such locations. The present example may be a case in point, for the giant in our photographs is one of the famous old trees of Long Island, New York, where it grows in a flat, sandy, apparently summer-baked site with no water of any kind within range of one's eyes.

Most kinds of trees have characteristic shapes from which they diverge markedly only as a result of storm damage, crowding, or some other adversity. Not so with the Pepperidge, incurable individualist that it is. Many times, in its earlier years, it forms an astonishingly symmetrical, sharply pointed pyramid nearly as broad as it is high, with all but the topmost branches virtually horizontal. Again, its top will be almost as flat as a floor, as if all desire to reach skyward had been crushed out of it by an overwhelming weight. On some older trees, too, all except the upper branches droop mournfully earthward, creating an appearance of utter dejection in sharp contrast with the evident courage of a sister tree but a few yards away.

Running through all these and other individual types, of course, are the threads of certain characteristic traits. Prominent among them are the rigidity and fantastic zigzaggedness of all the branches, clearly evident in the accompanying winter portrait. The reason? Well, I sometimes wonder if it may not lie in the cross-grained character of the tough, heavy, self-willed wood underneath that gray or pale brown bark.

Another invariable characteristic appears in the autumn when the thick, glossy, deep green leaves glow with shades of red so rich and varied that only the Swamp Maples and Sumachs can hope to equal them. As this gorgeous show begins the myriad blue-black fruits, single-pitted and sour to the taste, ripen into a feast for hosts of neighborhood birds from robins and flickers to waxwings, vireos, and sleek gray catbirds.

It is the seeds in these fruits that provide the tree's chief means of propagation, though some old specimens also send up suckers from the roots which, unless they are cut down, can soon develop into a large brood of offspring. Birds frequently disperse the seeds widely, and a few nurserymen use them to build up salable stocks of young trees. Even a small specimen grown in the wild is notoriously difficult to transplant, but the situation is different where the seeds are germinated under controlled conditions and the little trees are root-pruned and otherwise subjected to good nursery practices. A splendid demonstration of man's helpfulness in these ways are the dozens of fine Pepperidges in the Rochester (New York) City Parks, virtually all of them originating from seeds started by the Park Department, grown along in nursery rows, and ultimately set out in their permanent positions with virtually no loss. Seeing the locations assigned to them—some in hollows, others high on the rolling hills, and all thriving splendidly—you realize that the species is not nearly so choosy as many people have believed.

Where there is space for its proper development—and remember that ultimately it may attain a height and spread of 70 feet—there are few more worth-while deciduous ornamental trees than this adaptable and fully winter-hardened American. Insect pests and diseases bother it little if at all. Pruning is seldom necessary except for cutting occasional branches that may sweep so low as to interfere with the enjoyment of its welcome summer shade, and its change of pace as the seasons come and go is never monotonous.

Perhaps the day will come when more good tree nurseries will offer seed-grown trees, but you need not wait for that if you can get a handful of wild seeds yourself and sow them this fall an

inch deep in a protected, well-drained outdoor corner or a shaded coldframe where they will be safe until germination begins sometime next year. Actual freezing of the seeds will do no harm; on the contrary, it is usually an advantage. Once started, the young trees grow fairly rapidly and should be transplanted at least twice before you set them in permanent locations, so as to develop compact root systems.

123

WESTERN JUNIPER

It is one of the minor oddities of modern American life that so many of us should think of the West as a new, undeveloped country. Actually, the early civilizations of Mexico and parts of the Southwest are far older than any traceable human records that have been discovered in the East. And as far as living trees are concerned, you would have to search a long, long time to find anywhere on the New York side of the Plains a single one of any species whose age approaches that of the Redwood, the Giant Sequoia, or the Western Juniper (*Juniperus occidentalis*) which is the subject of this sketch.

This picturesque relative of our common Red-cedar is known to live for at least 1,100 years, and probably much longer. It is primarily a mountaineer, native to the slopes and elevated plains at altitudes of 6,000 to 10,000 feet in Washington, Oregon, and western Idaho down through the Sierra Nevadas to California's San Bernardino Range. It is naturally a low, broad-headed tree with horizontal, sturdy branches and unusually thick trunk, and is capable of reaching a height of 50 feet or so under unusually favorable circumstances. As a rule, though, it is incredibly distorted by the rigors of the lands it lives in, battered and twisted by the gales, scorched by rampant forest fires, crushed and broken by many feet of winter snows. Like the famous Monterey Cypress of the California coast, it lives by hanging on and fighting back, refusing to succumb or even yield to the elements and paying for its temerity with the battle scars of an old, old warrior.

Western Junipers are slow-growing trees, given to anchoring their roots deeply in the crevices of rocky ledges whence not even

the strongest gales can budge them. Good soil, to them, is the sort of gritty stuff that gardeners call barren, but they seem to like it. Where the reddish bark is sufficiently protected it grows to a thickness of half an inch, covering soft, light, close-grained wood, pale red-brown in color and extraordinarily durable when in contact with the soil. In these wood characteristics lies another true Juniper trait which may have a bearing on the great age that the tree attains. The accompanying close-up photograph of the trunk shows two interesting conditions often found in a very old tree: a great "muscle" of live, bark-covered wood swelling upward from the ground at the lower left; and on either side of it bare, weathered wood that was killed by fire long ago.

Despite the gnarled character of so many of the trees, Western Juniper wood is of considerable value for fencing posts and as fuel. The shreddy bark, too, was woven into cloth and mats by the Indians many years before the era of nylon and miracle plastics, and the tree's quarter-inch "berries" are still a food item among California tribes.

Most of us think of all evergreens as cone-bearers, producing small, flaky seeds between numerous rounded scales which, at maturity, separate and permit the seeds to escape. But the Western Juniper, like the rest of its group, departs sharply from this general pattern and provides for posterity by forming bony, wingless seeds enclosed in somewhat bluish, berry-like covers which actually consist of cone scales that have thickened and grown together. In most cases the more or less pulpy character of these tiny containers makes them edible so that they constitute an important food for a variety of wild birds. Each fruit of the Western Juniper is no longer than ⅓ inch and contains but two or three actual seeds, but the crop is so abundant that the total seed output is considerable.

Despite the hardships of the life it leads, the future of this Far Western Juniper seems reasonably secure. The ruggedness of its native region is actually a double safeguard, for it leads to distortions of growth that nullify much of the commercial value of the wood and, of course, effectively discourages lumbering operations on any considerable scale. So, barring some unforeseen calamity, these fantastically enduring trees will surmount the hardships of their mountain fastnesses for many another century.

127

CALIFORNIA
LIVE OAK

There are really two kinds of Live Oaks native to California: *Quercus agrifolia*, the one pictured here, and another, *Quercus chrysolepis*. The most noticeable differences are that the leaves of the former are a little larger and its acorns much more slender and smaller-cupped than those of the latter. Both species are evergreen, but their habitats are quite different, chrysolepis definitely preferring the mountain gulches and rocky canyons from Lower California northward into Oregon, while agrifolia is so addicted to the lower altitudes that it is often called the Coast Live Oak. In the southern half of the state it even extends its range to the islands lying off the mainland.

This Coast Live Oak is a massive tree, occasionally reaching a height of 100 feet. Oddly enough, it sometimes assumes a shrubby form, as though it had changed its mind about becoming a real tree. Normally, however, it is short-trunked and broad-limbed, a picturesque giant that inevitably gives the impression of flinging its arms abroad to provide welcome shade and shelter for as many sunbaked creatures as it can. You cannot but marvel that the great weight of these ponderous limbs does not wrench them loose where they join the trunk, but that seldom seems to happen. No doubt the explanation lies in the traditional strength of the wood, a characteristic found in all Oaks the world over. In addition to this,

the directional arrangement and grouping of the wood fibers at the junction point of any large branch and the trunk are splendidly calculated to withstand the extra strain put upon them by the laws of leverage and gravitation.

Live Oak leaves the world over, including those of *Quercus virginiana*, the species that is so notable in our southern states from Virginia to Mexico, are rather similar in over-all character. Thus this California species' foliage is a slightly grayish green, lighter and more glossy on the under side than on the upper surface. It is very persistent, so that the tree is well clothed throughout the winter. The effect is not spectacular, but singularly restful; indeed, few tree leaves can match those of the Live Oak for quiet dignity. Only in the spring, when the old foliage gives way to new successors, does the tree lose any of this peculiar charm, but that stage soon passes.

Commercially the Coast Live Oak is not too important, for though its wood is hard and durable, the extremely short trunk prevents cutting boards of any real length. Even the largest limbs are so irregular as to be of little value for lumber. The wood is good for fuel, to be sure, but in mild climates that is not a particularly important factor. Few tree lovers can regret these "shortcomings," for it would be a tragedy if the profit system of the lumberman were ever to threaten the welfare of such an impressive tree.

All trees have their queer little side lights, I suppose, some of them in their own ways of existence, and others involving the habits of other forms of life. I can think of none more odd, though, than is recorded in one photograph illustrating these comments. At a quick glance it may look as if someone had fired a load of buckshot into an old tree; but actually the holes were drilled in very thick, corky bark by California woodpeckers so as to provide receptacles in which they can cache Live Oak acorns for a future food supply. You will notice that each cavity is just about large enough to hold a single acorn firmly, and that several of them have been filled by the birds. And if you look closely, you will see that every nut has been inserted point first, leaving the round, relatively soft cup end exposed. No one ever told the woodpeckers that this is the most vulnerable point at which to peck into the nut's meaty interior—no one, that is, except Old Lady Nature, and she must have taught the lesson a long time ago!

131

DOUGLAS-FIR

To see this mighty evergreen at its best you must go to the mountains and coastal regions of the Northwest. There, despite the ravages of lumbermen, vast areas still remain where the trees stand close like the stalks in a gigantic wheat field, their butts sometimes 10 feet thick, their trunks rising straight as masts to tapered tops 200 feet or more above the ground. Next to the Redwood and Sequoia, the Douglas-fir (*Pseudotsuga taxifolia*) ranks as America's tallest tree. And out in that expansive country which is its native home you will find many people who enthusiastically claim that its stature, coupled with its ridged red-brown bark, close-ranked needles, and pendent cones, make it the handsomest of all living trees.

It was the famous Scottish plant hunter, David Douglas, who introduced this towering conifer to the outside world nearly 125 years ago when he returned to Portsmouth with a supply of seeds gathered during a three-year exploration of what was then an all but unknown wilderness. Through the intervening years it has been widely established not only in other portions of northern North America but also in Europe. Fast-growing, easily raised from seed, tough of wood, and handsome in every stage, it has been well termed "a tree for the million."

The Douglas-fir is native in many parts of the Rockies from central British Columbia southward to the Mexican border. The wide area over which it grows presents many variations in climate, with corresponding differences in the size of the trees and the quality of their tan-yellow wood from the lumber standpoint. The best grades furnish masts for ships, piles for dock building and other long-log construction work, for they are hard and probably the strongest provided by any American conifer. Great quantities are cut into boards and other building-size lumber, though they often have a tendency to warp and are too hard for easy cutting and fitting. Railroad ties and posts account for much of the timber that the lumbermen cut, for the wood stands up well under exposure.

Experiments with seeds gathered from these different geographical strains have shown that certain characteristics of the parent trees are handed down to their offspring. Seedlings originating in the higher parts of the northern Rockies can stand considerably colder climates than their coastal region counterparts, which obviously has greatly broadened the establishment of the species in other parts of the world.

Botanically, Douglas-firs stand between the true Firs and the Spruces, with some of the technical characteristics of each. Their branches primarily grow horizontally, with some variations both upward and downward. The needles are ¾ inch or more in length, lively green above and blue-white beneath, a two-tone effect made still more attractive by the yellowish or tan surface of the young twigs from which they grow so thickly.

Trees that produce great quantities of vigorous seeds naturally tend to form forests, and the Douglas-fir is no exception. A typical stand of it is so dense that all other kinds are crowded out and the high canopy of boughs keeps the forest floor in perpetual semi-dusk. No doubt this crowding bears heavily on the height of the trees, for their competition to keep their heads in the sun must be strenuous indeed. Such close companionship, too, is the reason for the absence of branches on the lower half or more of the trunks. By contrast, a tree that has grown up in the open forms a broad-based pyramid of marked regularity and beauty, much less slender than the forest-grown specimens.

Ideally, these mighty conifers should have a rich, somewhat moist soil and a climate which is by no means arid. Here and there, however, in such dry regions as Kansas and Nebraska, they have been introduced with worth-while success by planting in wind-sheltered places and providing mutual protection by putting them in groups rather than more or less isolated single specimens. It cannot be expected, though, that any climate appreciably different from the one to which they have been accustomed for countless centuries will promote their finest development.

FLOWERING DOGWOOD

According to the botanists there are a dozen or more different species of Dogwood native to the United States, but there is just one which we plain gardeners instantly think of whenever we hear the word mentioned: it's that spectacular, aristocratic, and wholly endearing Flowering Dogwood (*Cornus florida*) which every spring when the world is turning green again, spreads its blossom tiers through countless woodlands in the eastern half of the United States. Seeing it thus, you need no second glance to understand its rating as our finest early-season flowering tree.

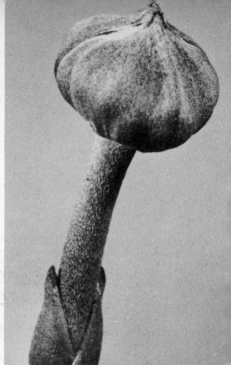

Normally this leader of the native Dogwood clan never exceeds a height of 40 feet, and most of the mature ones you see are between 20 and 30 feet tall. Barring accident, it is a one-trunk, fairly straight tree with widely spaced, somewhat horizontal branches bearing numerous upcurved twigs at the tips of which the blossoms are borne. In woodlands it tends to be irregular, though always interesting in outline, but in uncrowded surroundings it can be wide-spreading and well proportioned.

At every season of the year the Flowering Dogwood is an exceptionally rewarding ornamental tree. Its most famous show, of course, comes in spring with the expanding of the four (usually) great white or pink-tinged bracts surrounding each cluster of tiny yellowish-green true flowers. By the time these pass their prime the sage-green points of the new foliage are well advanced, and quickly the tree becomes clothed with handsome, broadly oval leaves as much as 5 or 6 inches long. All summer they are lovely in their two-tone effect—rich green above, lighter and silvered below—and then, in late September, come the first signs of the deep purple-

wine tones which gradually overspread all the leaves and form an unbelievable background for the countless clusters of little scarlet fruits at the twig tips.

How the migrating birds love to feast on those glowing seeds, and with what determination the remnants of the colorful leaf army defy the sharp frosts even into November before loosening their hold and eddying to earth! Then with the vanishing of the last of those bright traces the tree stands in softer and far different beauty, a color harmony of subtle mauves and lavenders dotted with the wee gray button buds of next spring's blossoms. On every sunny day that follows, these quiet colors glow with suppressed life, as lovely a sight as a discerning eye can find in all the winter woods. Though the mercury may crowd the zero mark, the Dogwood never fails to look as though spring were really just around the corner.

It is not generally realized that the four broad "petals" which have brought such fame to the Dogwood's blossoms are not petals at all, but merely the expanded winter coverings of the flower bud. When they first unfold they are tiny and yellow-green, and

their darker, slightly deformed tips show clearly that only a short time before they were locked together to form the points of the unopened buds. As the bracts grow rapidly larger, though, their color pales until, at the time of greatest expansion, it becomes the typical pure white. But still the very tips retain that twisted look inherited from their months of exposure to the elements.

I have mentioned that sometimes the bracts show a tinge of pink or rose—apparently a peculiarity of individual trees, and therefore subject to considerable variation in intensity. In certain sections of the country this deepening of color is especially prevalent and pronounced, and it is from trees in which this change was most marked that the so-called pink Dogwood probably originated by nursery grafting or budding on seedlings of the ordinary type. Personally, I think that most of the nurserymen doing this work must be singularly lacking in good taste or else are downright color-blind, for the average "pink" Dogwood offered for sale has about as muddy, mongrelish, and homely a color as you could imagine. One of these days, perhaps, some grower will offer trees derived from some of the lovely blush-pink-tinted wild forms and make a real hit with discriminating gardeners. Perhaps even now attempts are being made to establish good natural pink strains by seed sowing and selection.

Why a plant genus as lovely as the Dogwoods has been given such an uninspired sort of common name is something of an enigma. The most plausible explanation I have heard is that the bark of one of the European species, well boiled in water to produce a strong decoction, was once used as a wash for mangy dogs —certainly a practical purpose, if not exactly esthetic. In any event, the term is applied nowadays to all species, whether tree-like, as in the case of the one discussed here, or the shrubby types which form the majority of the group.

Flowering Dogwood is naturally a very prolific tree—a fortunate fact, considering the vandal-mindedness of that considerable section of mankind to whom the sight of attractive blossoms is an open invitation to ruin their parent by chopping, ripping, and tearing loose whole branches of them. The hard-coated seeds— one of them inside each of the little red fruits—germinate so freely that the woodland ground near a fair-sized tree, if undisturbed for a few years, is quite sure to be plentifully dotted with seedlings of various sizes. Much wider distribution, too, is accomplished by the birds.

In ordinary woods where these volunteer seedlings are numerous only a small percentage of them are likely to amount to much as display trees later on because of the checks on their development that result from the crowding of other growths, so it is permissible to transplant a few of the smaller ones in spring and give them a better chance for survival on your own grounds. Even though only a foot tall, their typical Dogwood leaves are a reliable identifying mark, and so are the distinctive bark and the twig habit.

It is perfectly simple to grow your own trees from seed—literally by the hundred, if you wish to—though six or seven years will probably elapse between sowing and the first blossoms. Gather the fruits when they have attained their full scarlet coloring, soak them in water for several days to macerate the pulp, rub out the seeds by "scouring" between layers of burlap or other coarse cloth, sow from ½ to ¾ inch deep in a flat that can be stored for the.

winter in some shaded, unheated, mouseproof place. Many of the seeds will germinate the following spring; others may delay for an additional year. Transplant the youngsters when their first true leaves are well out, and thereafter as their increasing stature suggests. If this seems too tedious a project, cheer up, for Flowering Dogwoods grow quite fast, especially while young.

This five-star flowering tree is exceptionally useful in home-grounds landscaping. It will do well in just about any type of soil, provided it is well drained and of reasonably good quality. Full sunlight is conducive to maximum flowering, as with so many other plants, but a fair amount of bloom develops where there is considerable shade—even as much as three fourths. You cannot escape the fact, though, that a shaded location makes for a much more straggly growth form than the same tree would develop if it had been living in full, open light. Transplanting is best done in early spring before visible growth starts.

Diseases and insect pests? Well, the only serious trouble of this nature that I have come across is borers—and these are serious! In some regions the borers are quite prevalent and are more likely to be in wild trees collected from the woods than in nursery-grown specimens that have been properly cared for. If there is an adequate method of coping with a real borer invasion, I've never heard of it. A few of the pests, though, which are most likely to attack the trunk and larger branches, can be pretty well managed by discovering the "frass" or "sawdust" that marks their workings and injecting one of the several borer preparations which are offered by the good garden supply stores. Sometimes you can skewer a borer and put an end to his evil days by pushing a thin, flexible wire into the tunnel entrance and probing around industriously.

There is a fanciful tale to the effect that the Dogwood's snowy flowers date from the spring day when Pierrot, climbing a ladder to brighten up the moon's face with whitewash, accidentally tipped his bucket high in the sky and spattered the trees below with its contents. Well, that's the sort of irresponsible thing Pierrot would have done, for he was a featherbrained fellow. But whitewash—no, a commonplace thing like that just couldn't ever be connected with anything as perfect as Flowering Dogwood!

143

LONG-LEAF
PINE

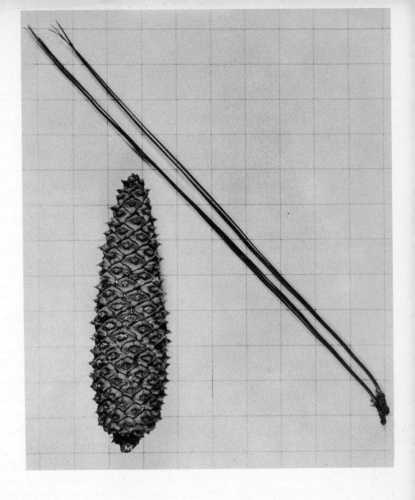

If you know your coastal Southland from Norfolk to upper Florida and westward into Alabama, the splendid "horsetail" branch tips of this famous tree are sure to be among your best-loved associations. No other Pine native to the United States, I suspect, can match the unique beauty of these superb 3-foot plumes of bright olive-green needles, some of them 18 inches long, so showy and flexible that you cannot resist the temptation to swish them through the air just to hear the clean, sibilant sound they make. And if that is not enough, there are the showy red- and blue-tinted staminate flower spikes in spring, the 8-inch cones at the branch tips, and the unforgettable fountain forms of the young seedlings rising here and there from the silent floor of fallen needles under the old parent trees.

The first time I saw a stand of Long-leaves (*Pinus palustris*) at close range was years ago in Alabama, and the space between their scattered seedling cascades was sprinkled with deep blue bird's-foot violets. From ground to feathery treetops fifty feet above there was no single lapse in the succession of perfect color harmonies.

The Long-leaf (Georgia Pine, Turpentine Pine, and Southern Yellow Pine are other common names for it) is a tree of marked economic as well as ornamental importance in the South. Its sap is a primary source of commercial rosin and turpentine, and its hard, close-grained, tough, and handsome ocher-to-orange-colored wood is famous for its structural as well as decorative value; foot for foot, it is almost twice as heavy as the wood of White Pine.

Long-leaf Pines have been known to grow 100 feet high and develop trunk diameters of 4 feet, though the usual dimensions are considerably below these figures. The trunk is notably straight, and often, when the trees are more or less crowded, entirely free of branches on its lower half, so that the reddish-brown, thin-scaled plates of the bark are a prominent and pleasing feature. Such a high location of the branches minimizes their effect of coarseness, which is not at all objectionable even in the case of isolated "specimen" trees whose branches begin at a much lower point.

I have never been able to decide whether I like the Long-leaf Pine best as a "colony" tree or as a single specimen out in the open. There is something calm and immensely satisfying about the clean, needle-cushioned floor of a Pine woods that nothing else can supply, and the scattered ranks of column-like trunks that support the high, almost mist-like ceiling lose none of their impressiveness even after familiarity has worn their novelty thin. An isolated single tree cannot, in the very nature of things, provide these effects, but on the other hand, its appearance of vigorous health is much more evident, and the beauty of its form and more numerous individual branches cannot be matched by the majority of woods-growing trees. From the home-grounds standpoint the choice between grove and specimen use hinges largely, I suppose, on the amount of space you have available and the particular effect you want.

If you should decide that you'd like to plant Long-leaf Pines, better be sure, first, that you are at least reasonably close to the regions of the tree's natural range as outlined in the beginning of this sketch; and second, that you can provide the sort of dry, sandy location that the species likes. Most nurseries do not offer stock of it since it is generally considered a timber tree rather than an ornamental. In case you fail to locate a suitable commercial source it may be possible for you to collect small seedlings from the wild, or arrange with someone to do it for you. As with most evergreens, early spring is the most favorable season for transplanting.

COTTONWOOD

Strictly speaking, the Cottonwood (*Populus deltoidea*) and the Carolina Poplar (*Populus canadensis*) are two different trees, but they are so closely related that in the popular mind their common names are often used interchangeably. Both are Poplars, of course, with numerous similarities, but the true Cottonwood, to which these pages are devoted, is larger and more spreading than its cousin and, to my way of thinking, a far superior tree. In one or more almost identical forms, it ranges all the way from Quebec to Florida and westward to the Rockies—a big home for a big tree, and not too easy a one to occupy with distinction.

Though I have known the Cottonwood well and widely since early boyhood, I find it puzzling to define exactly the appeal it makes to so many thousands of Americans. The sheer majesty of the tree, towering sometimes 150 feet above the rich bottom lands where it reaches its finest development, is one part of the story, to be sure, and another is found in the great boon of the summer shade cast by its millions of neat, smooth green leaves that twinkle so cheerily on their flattened stems with every passing breeze. Perhaps these two assets, coupled with the racial habit of rapid growth, are sufficient cause for fame, but there are some of us to whom its clouds of "cotton" floating afar through the joyousness of a bright May day are the final touch of Cottonwood charm. Yes, I know that these snowy, drifting powder puffs with their treasure of seeds from the female tree are a nuisance when they blow against the window screens, and that the fallen catkins clutter up the lawn and walks under the trees that bear them. But these are only minor and temporary conditions that are of small moment when compared with the proof they bring that spring has really come.

Cottonwood has the reputation of being a brittle tree, for its wood is light and soft. Actually, it often does suffer considerable branch breakage when growing in windy locations, but the rapidity with which new growth is made replaces such damage surprisingly fast, and the net result is that many an old specimen still retains an acceptably symmetrical form. The winter photograph of the tree demonstrates clearly these two factors of breakage and repair.

Commercially, the wood of the Poplar tribe, including Cottonwood, is used chiefly for papermaking and the construction of boxes, and so is of considerable importance. It does not, however, rate economically with the Oaks and some of the timber-type conifers, such as Pines and Firs. The wood itself is a very pale brown, and the bark which covers it, while gray-green and quite smooth in the case of young trees, roughens with age and gradually becomes brown. The twig bark, regardless of the size of the tree, is a pleasant shade of ocher-yellow.

In some parts of the country Cottonwoods have been extensively planted as windbreaks and to provide shade and greenery along streets and highways. As ornamental trees for home grounds, though, they are not too highly rated, chiefly because of their potential great size and the nuisance of branch breakage and springtime untidiness already mentioned. On large properties, of course, these drawbacks are less important, and under such conditions the tree really comes into its own. Somehow it never seems quite at home in cramped surroundings, despite the fact that, from the purely cultural angle, few tree species are better fitted to withstand the difficult conditions of city locations.

My favorite Cottonwood tree lifts its crown over a hundred feet above a wee cove of fat meadowland all but surrounded by the rugged, rocky hills of lower New York State. To the west, north, and east those forested slopes raise a thousand-foot barrier against the

winds, and for many, many years this old Cottonwood has looked out placidly across the southward valley flatlands as if supremely contented in the security of its protecting hills.

Summer days can be hot in that country, but in all the many times that I have followed the gin-clear trout stream which romps down from the heights and past the mouth of the cove, it has been pleasant under the big tree. There is an old well there, and the cellar hole of a long-vanished farmhouse, and even in the most breathless noontide a stir of cool air from the waterside flows across them and on into the woods beyond. Sometimes a bit of breeze from the main valley joins it, and then the Cottonwood's leaves dance playfully, and the rustle of their movements is restful beyond all describing. For a hundred years, perhaps, the stream and the tree and the hills have been companions, the moods of one the moods of all. Out of such companionships, perhaps, infinitely varied across the land and so often linked with the lives of men, grows one more reason why the Cottonwood deserves its place among America's best-loved trees.

151

WILLOW
OAK

Judged by some of its accepted family standards, the Willow Oak (*Quercus phellos*) might be some carelessly adopted child, for its leaves look far more like a Willow's than an Oak's. As the accompanying photograph suggests, they are lance-like and wholly devoid of the prominent lobes and indentations so generally associated with other members of the genus. But the structure of the tree is rather Oak-like, and the relationship is still more clearly demonstrated by the pendent springtime flowers and the unmistakable acorns which mature from them two years later.

This quick-growing, rather unconventional Oak is something of a southerner and a justly popular shade tree, especially in cities and towns. The immediate vicinity of New York City seems to be the northern limit of its natural range, and it becomes more common as you go south along the Atlantic coast to Florida. The Gulf States are the real center of its abundance and beauty, and from them it extends northward, on the west side of the Appalachians, into Arkansas and the lower parts of Missouri, Tennessee, and Kentucky. So long as the climate suits it, you may find it thriving in a variety of situations from rich, moist lowland to sandy flats.

Most kinds of Oaks have hard wood, but that of the Willow, while strong and quite heavy, is softer than that of its relatives. Commercially I doubt if it has great value, though I am told that to some extent it is used for making wheel hubs and boxes, and, like almost any reasonably good wood, in general building construction. All in all, it is as an excellent ornamental that the tree has gained its chief popularity.

To see a well-grown Willow Oak is to realize at once why it is so highly prized. Few spreading shade trees are more symmetrical in outline or better balanced in their relationship of trunk and branch areas. When the leaves have yellowed and dropped after their season's service, too, the whole framework of the tree looks both strong and graceful with a nice tapering of diameters from base to branch tips. A particularly fine specimen may reach a height of 60 feet or more, with a similar branch spread and a trunk diameter of 4 feet. All of which comprises quite a full-scale shade tree, anywhere and any time.

It is obvious from these dimensional figures that, if you are considering your home tree planting from a long-range viewpoint, Wil-

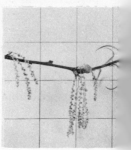

low Oaks can be a splendid choice for large grounds but a poor one for small areas. As for the maintenance question, it seldom poses any great problem, for neither diseases nor insect pests are likely to be serious enough to call for more than standard control measures; indeed, they may never bother a Willow Oak enough to be noticeable.

As in virtually all kinds of tree planting, nursery-grown specimens are the best because of their superior shape and the condition of their root systems. Trees less than 15 feet tall are the easiest to move and quickest to take hold in their new locations, and late fall, winter, and early spring are the preferred moving seasons. Good soil, firm planting, generous watering, and adequate support to keep the trunk vertical until new root formation insures its staying so are the concluding moves to get a new Willow Oak off to a good start.

HORSE-CHESTNUT

Few tree tribes are so picturesquely named as the Buckeyes, or Horse-chestnuts, for their large brown nuts do suggest the eyes of a deer, and certainly the prefix "horse" implies that these "chestnuts" are not the kind that humans like to eat.

Altogether, there are about twenty members of this genus, ranging from 80-foot trees down to moundlike shrubs no taller than a man. Through them all, though, run certain similar traits—thick-husked nuts, large compound leaves grouped in clusters somewhat like the fingers of a hand ("digitate," as the botanists described them), and prominent, often showy blossom spires at the ends of the twigs.

In many parts of the country the best-known Horse-chestnut is the one presented on the following pages, *Aesculus hippo-castanum*. Long ago it was introduced to this country from abroad, and through the years it has spread so widely, with man's help as well as by its own self-feeding, that today it has practically the status of a truly native American. One suspects that successive generations of our boys and girls have played no small part in this extension of range, for those shiny nuts are perfect ammunition for throwing at various targets!

This particular Horse-chestnut may ultimately reach a height of 70 feet or more, but rarely will you find one of such stature. Usually the trunk divides into several strong, ascending limbs 10 or 15 feet from the ground, building a framework for the tree's characteristic oval, well-filled outline. Heavy twigs and dull brown bark increase its rugged look.

From the display standpoint, the high tide of the Horse-chestnut's year comes in the latter part of spring, when its branches bear broad, showy spires of white blossoms tinged red and with yellow stamens that curve outward well beyond the corolla rim.

This is the stage in which most of us recall it, but there are other seasons when its individuality is quite as marked, though less obvious. All winter, for example, its upcurved twigs are tipped with great brown buds that glisten as if they were coated with varnish. As spring approaches, a new brightness comes to them, and with the arrival of warm days they swell and open their scales to reveal the leaf bundles packed ingeniously in silky gray down. Almost overnight, it seems, these leaves unfold to clothe the tree with silvery green tents that soon become open umbrellas and, darkening, cast heavy shade below. In this last phase the memorable blossom show is staged.

This particular Buckeye species has been widely planted for generations along our streets and highways and as a shade and ornamental lawn tree. However, it is far from being a perfect choice for such places, for during the growing season it quite constantly has the untidy habit of dropping things. First the bud scales fall and litter the ground in spring, and then the flowers follow suit. Many of the spiny nut-bearing burrs drop before they are ripe, and often during the summer a combination of dry weather and overcrowding causes a good many leaves to die and sail earthward. Yet, despite these shortcomings, Horse-chestnuts have their days of high triumph.

PONDEROSA PINE

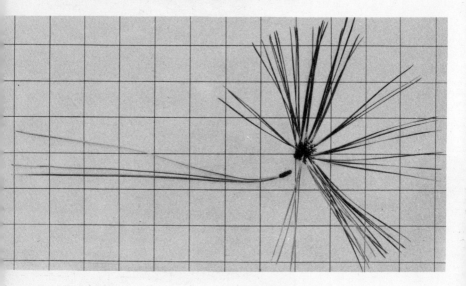

This is the famous Yellow Pine of the West, standing in countless thousands from British Columbia and Montana south to western Nebraska, Texas, and California. In the dryish foothills of southern Oregon *Pinus ponderosa* lifts its handsome yellow-green crown 150 feet or more above the volcanic soil, and magnificent forests of it clothe the rich westward slopes of the coast mountains clear down to the Mexican border from 2,500 feet altitude up to timber line. Of all the Pines it is the most adaptable, accepting with good grace dry air or moist, rich soil or sterile. Small wonder that it rates as one of the most valuable lumber trees of the Far West and Southwest, for its hard, strong wood, ranging in color from pale yellow to almost terra-cotta red, has many commercial uses and can be cut in large sizes.

"Majesty" is a trite word and often abused, yet none other so well describes a fine specimen of this straight-stemmed, short-branched evergreen at the peak of its 400-year life. At breast height its trunk may have a diameter of 6 feet or more, and the red-brown, broadly plated bark which clothes it has a rugged beauty worth going far to see. Typically its stout branches grow at a downward

angle, but their ends turn upward in a way that more than counteracts any suggestion of dreariness or discouragement. The green and purple cones they bear are splendidly displayed against the shining background of the needles. The whole effect is one of virile health.

It was the famous Scottish plant explorer David Douglas who suggested the name "ponderosa" to describe the great size of the tree and, perhaps, that density of its wood which in our earlier lumbering days made it necessary for the huge logs to be dried for several months before they could be floated down the rivers on their way to the mills. Douglas, however, was not the one who originally brought the species to the attention of the world; that distinction belongs to the Lewis and Clark expedition.

Ponderosas have a number of geographical forms, a fact which may account in part for the considerable variations in the length of the needles from 4 to 8 inches and in the color of the wood itself; even the bark, in some cases, is blackish rather than red. As the scientists continue to study their differences, it may be that some will become technically classified as distinct species, an analytical distinction which will hardly alter the fact that in the public's eye they are all Ponderosas.

For all its adaptability to varying conditions through the vast area in which it is native, the Ponderosa Pine does only moderately well where it has been introduced in the eastern states and in Europe. In these unaccustomed lands its growth is slow, and there is doubt that it would ever reach anything like its impressive normal height. The general outline, too, is radically altered, as witness the photograph on the opposite page of one that has been growing for many years on an estate in lower New York State.

Perhaps, after all, we should be satisfied with enjoying the Ponderosa among the mountains that it loves so well, without trying to force it to grow elsewhere. It is one of the most splendid, all but unbelievable sights of the Far West, an impressive symbol of America's natural productiveness. In these days when the world is so obsessed by the stupidities and errors that bring tumult into the affairs of men, there may well be a lesson as well as a pleasure in going quietly through the western Yellow Pine forests and seeing how infinitely Nature surpasses us in maintaining balance among the multitudes.

161

CALIFORNIA
BUCKEYE

Whether you call it Buckeye or Horse-chestnut is rather a matter of local usage and personal preference, because both are correct from the botanical standpoint. To most people the former ·term indicates the lower-growing, broad, and sometimes shrubby members of the clan, while the latter is applied to the taller, regular tree types. All, of course, have many characteristics in common, most striking of which are the leaves, blossoms, and large brown nuts which are said to look somewhat like a deer's eye.

California Buckeyes (*Aesculus californica*) are usually impressively broad, rounded trees that ultimately reach a height of 30 to 40 feet; only occasionally do they develop a shrub-like character. On branches and twigs their bark is smooth and gray, a thoroughly pleasing combination, but on the trunk of a good-sized specimen it shows rough with age. Few trees are more interesting at a distance in their leafless season, when the innumerable massed twigs seem to invest the entire contour with a pale, soft haze of great loveliness as the sunlight brings out its full tones.

Spring marks the start of the Buckeye's real show. First the tip buds swell and open to release the several compound leaves, each of the five leaflets drooping modestly from a common center so that the tree seems decked with a multitude of nearly closed umbrellas. This stage passes rapidly as the foliage expands, and almost before

you know it the whole tree is alight with white to pale rose flower spires set against a rich green background. From this stage until the leaves fall in autumn the tree casts an unusually dense shade—one of its most welcome features in regions where summer days can be really hot.

Easterners accustomed to associating Horse-chestnut fruits with picturesquely rough and horny husks will be surprised to find that the outer coverings of this West Coast species are entirely without projecting points. But the family likeness is strong indeed when the shining, rich brown nuts themselves are exposed—generally one, sometimes two, inside each husk.

The California Buckeye is native to the low hills and canyon sides of the Coast Range and the Sierra Nevadas. Its normal limit seems to be the upper Sacramento Valley, and from there you will find it growing wild as far south as Los Angeles County. In cultivation, of course, its range is considerably greater, but attempts to establish it in other states where the winter climate is definitely more rugged are seldom successful because it simply cannot stand really cold weather.

This California species is one of the best Buckeyes for home-grounds planting and could well be used to a great extent in the Middle and Deep South regions of the East. It grows readily enough from seeds sown in the autumn and presents no particular cultural difficulties. Like others of its race, it likes ample sunlight and space to expand laterally, as well as a loamy, reasonably moist soil. Apparently the British appreciate its landscaping value more than we do, for long ago they introduced it as a home-grounds tree on their side of the ocean. Showy flowering trees of comparable size are far from numerous—particularly those which can also offer such assets as abundant summer shade.

164

INCENSE-CEDAR

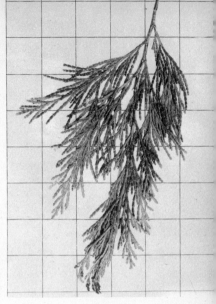

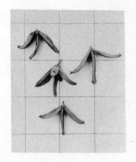

Botanically speaking, the Incense-cedars are allied to the Arbor-
vitaes. Theirs is a small clan of evergreens—only about nine species
in all, mostly hailing from such far-flung lands as New Zealand,
Chile, Patagonia, China, and Formosa. Here in the United States
only this one is native (*Libocedrus decurrens*), and even at that
its natural territory is limited to the Coast Ranges from Oregon
to Lower California. Whenever you see it growing in the East or
in Europe, you can be sure that it has been introduced. Indeed,
introduced or not, it is the only species of the group that could
stand the winter climate of the northeastern states.

A really mature specimen at its best may be nearly 200 feet tall,
with a lower trunk diameter of 10 feet. In general appearance it
strongly suggests an Arborvitae, particularly in the frondlike, almost ferny character of its warm yellow-green foliage and the strip-
like appearance of the bright cinnamon bark. It never seems to
form great forests like those of the Ponderosa Pine; rather, you
find it scattered singly or in small groups among the other trees that
clothe the mountains between the 4,000- and 7,000-foot levels.

Winters are not too frigid in good Incense-cedar country, and
yet it is always a surprise to find these splendid trees tinged with
tiny flowers in January or February—the female ones pale green
and inconspicuous, the yellow males so numerous that their whole

effect calls to mind the plumes of a Goldenrod in full bloom. When seen above the snow on a sunny day, the effect is incredibly beautiful.

In its younger years, especially when growing strongly in the open, our Incense-cedar forms an almost geometrically perfect pyramid, its lower branches nearly touching the ground, and the whole mass so densely overlapping that it sheds both rain and snow. In old age, after battling the elements for perhaps a thousand years, it is far more irregular and picturesque, often with several summits trying to replace the old one destroyed long before by lightning or a great wind.

The seed-bearing cones of this handsome evergreen are scarcely an inch long, and wholly unlike those of a Pine or Spruce. Actually, they have only four woody scales instead of dozens of thin, flattish ones, and these flare out from a common base somewhat as do the petals of a flower. Two of them are usually sterile, and each of the others contains only a pair of winged seeds.

Incense-cedars are splendid park and large home-grounds trees in climates suitable for them. In the East they stand the winters fairly well as far north as New York City, and even in particularly sheltered spots in eastern Massachusetts. But to know them at their perfect best you really should make a trip to the sheltered canyons of the central California ranges and see for yourself.

166

CALIFORNIA LAUREL

Any plant capable of becoming a 90-foot tree or a 10-foot shrub merely through the influence of its environment is worthy of anyone's respect, but the California-laurel, California Bay, or Oregon-myrtle (*Umbellularia californica*) has far more claim to popular admiration than that. Through its natural range from southwestern Oregon through the Coast Ranges and Sierras to southern California, it is one of the handsomest and most characteristic trees of the region, a towering evergreen noted for its intrinsic beauty and the shade cast by its far-flung branches. This last asset, by the way, finds echo in the first half of its botanical name, derived from the Latin *umbrella*, meaning a sunshade. Actually, this similarity is said to refer to the form of the flower clusters, though personally I am willing to leave it to the botanists to point out the sunshade resemblance in that connection.

Whether you consider it as a whole or detail by detail, California-laurel is rich with special interest. Its narrow yellow-green leaves, from 3 to 5 inches long, remain on the tree for several years, and even while still green they will burn vigorously if tossed into a fire. From December to May it is decked with yellow-green fragrant flower clusters that lead later to little purple fruits not unlike king-sized editions of those of the Sassafras. Typically, the bark of large specimens is thin, dark brown, and scaly, but on smaller trees it is smoother and more grayish.

Structurally, the tree has slim, ascending branches that climb to

168

a rather narrow crown when hemmed in by near neighbors, but out in the open the shape is more rounded, the branches are heavier. All this is frequently forgotten when, under rugged conditions of soil and aridity, the growth becomes shrub-like. It is said that trees with a trunk diameter of 20 inches or so are from 150 to 200 years old, so evidently the species is a fairly slow grower. Regardless of size, its wood is hard, heavy, fine-grained, and rich brown, a combination which gives it value for the interior finishing of houses as well as cabinetwork.

To an easterner this favorite lawn and park tree of the West Coast is superficially reminiscent of the Willows, partly because it reaches its finest development in well-watered bottom lands and also because of the shape of its leaves. There, however, the resemblance ceases, for since the deciduous Willow is usually brittle and short-lived, the evergreen California-laurels are definitely enduring.

In those areas where, instead of becoming tree-like, this species grows in crowded, many-stemmed thickets, it should prove valuable as a tall hedge or living windbreak, especially if periodically sheared to encourage density and restrict the over-all height.

Not too much has been written in praise of the California-laurel, for some obscure reason. Perhaps the best tribute to it was that given by the peer of all tree judges, the late Professor Charles S. Sargent, who once described it as "one of the stateliest and most beautiful inhabitants of the North American forests, and no evergreen tree of temperate regions surpasses it in the beauty of its dark, dense crown of lustrous foliage and in the massiveness of habit which make it one of the most striking features of the California landscape."

LIVE
OAK

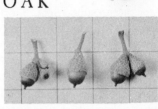

Our southern states are rich in handsome native tree species, but you must look far indeed to find any that can surpass the evergreen Live Oak (*Quercus virginiana*) for sheer picturesque effect. Short-trunked, gnarly of limb, and often draped with the ghostly gray beards of Spanish moss (*Tillandsia usneoides*), it is wholly un-oak-like to eyes accustomed to its northern relatives. Yet there at the twig tips are thousands of true little acorns, and if you could look beneath the reddish-brown bark you'd see typical Oak wood, durable, hard to cut, and amazingly heavy. Few other woods can take as high a polish when used for interior finish, and few can serve as well in the rugged job of bracing the sides of large boats.

Probably the Live Oak's chief claim to popular fame is its unique appearance as it approaches maturity. The main trunk, as I have said, is very short, and many of the massive, angular limbs which strike out from it have a horizontal tendency which, in old age, draws them into a position practically parallel to the ground. Eventually the tree may reach a height of 50 or even 75 feet, but so unusual is its manner of growth that a branch spread of double that distance is not unusual. Typically, an old specimen growing in an uncrowded place forms an amazingly broad-based dome, the most perfect shade tree in all the world. One wonders how such extended horizontal branches can support their own weight, not to mention the risk of splitting off at the trunk. But somehow they do meet the situation, and with little apparent sign of breakage. Probably the explanation of their success lies in the toughness of the wood fibers, coupled with changes in the direction of the grain at the numerous elbows and angles which even a very old limb shows.

In its lesser details, too, a Live Oak is in a class by itself. Its leaves, dark olive green above, paler and hoary below, are only from 2 to 4 inches long, and virtually devoid of the scalloped edges which we generally associate with the Oak genus. Toward the end of winter they gradually turn to brownish yellow and fall from the tree as the new crop appears in spring. This is the only part of the year when the tree fails to look its best, but it is not for long, and besides, there is always the grandeur of the branch framework. The acorns, even when ripe, are no more than two thirds of an inch long—neat dark brown mites deeply set in small-scaled, tightly fit-

ted caps attached to fuzzy stemlets. They reach full maturity by early autumn, from red-stigma flower spikes that open in the spring. The male or staminate flowers, in the usual Oak tradition, take the form of pendent catkins.

The so-called Spanish moss which is so prominent a part of the Live Oak's appearance is not a true Moss but is related to the Pineapple. Even thickly draped, its streamers seem to do trees no harm, despite the common erroneous belief that they are parasitic growths which necessarily sap the strength of the tree.

A tree with so many assets seems born to play an important role in ornamental plantings, therefore it is no wonder that the Live Oak is one of the South's most prized species for a wide variety of landscape uses. It grows rapidly, transplants easily, and lives long and healthily. From Virginia south along the coast and islands to Biscayne Bay, in Florida, westward along the Gulf Coast to the Rio Grande and inland into Texas it is especially prized as a specimen on good-sized home grounds as well as for avenue planting. Its preference is for sandy soil throughout this area, and also in those parts of Lower California, Cuba, and Central America to which its range extends. But even in this respect it is amenable to reason, so even though your soil is a bit on the heavy side the chances are a Live Oak won't resent it so long as the land is not waterlogged.

The fame of the Live Oak, naturally enough, extends far back into the history of the Deep South. Nearly two centuries ago Mark Catesby wrote that the Indians gathered its acorns "to thicken their venison-soop."

MONTEREY
CYPRESS

Of the seven members of the true Cypress clan which are native to the United States, the Monterey species (*Cupressus macrocarpa*) is by all odds the most famous. Not that it is more abundant than its cousins which occupy the general West Coast region. On the contrary, it is perhaps the rarest of the lot—in the wild state. Today its only known natural range is the coastal bluffs around California's Bay of Monterey, and even there it is losing ground as the shore line slowly recedes under the battering of the seas. Tree lovers can be thankful that it takes well to propagation and cultivation, for it is only a question of time until its final natural abode is washed out of existence.

It is the extreme picturesqueness of these remnants clinging grimly to what is left of their native home that accounts primarily for the tree's widespread fame. Distorted by the winds sweeping in from the Pacific, gnarled and stunted and deformed by age and the rigors of life in a region where the destructive elements of Nature battle unendingly to ruin what Nature herself has wrought, the Monterey Cypresses out there on the rim of the Pacific are the most fantastic-looking trees I have ever seen.

It would be idle to do more than speculate on the reasons why a tree which has proved itself adaptable to easier growing conditions in various parts of the world should have become so restricted in its natural range that, but for man's efforts to increase it, it would be headed for extinction. There appears to be no evidence that the human race set it on the downward course or that it has been the victim of some vast convulsion of Nature or change of climate. Perhaps it is just one of those species which never were really abundant or widespread, for reasons that have thus far escaped us.

Or it may be that, as the ecologists would say, it has passed its climax and has been marked for the discard by the laws of that slow, inexorable process which we call evolution.

The Monterey Cypress is an evergreen, of course, though its foliage is of the scale rather than the needle type, and the clustered plates which protect its seeds until maturity are hard and woody rather than thin as in the cones of Pines and Spruces. Under normally good conditions it develops into a symmetrical, dense, and pyramidal tree up to 70 feet or so in height, with a marked tendency for its crown to broaden out and become flatter with age. As this stage progresses the tree grows more gnarly and irregular, and its short trunk may attain a diameter of 5 or even 6 feet.

As to colors: the scale leaves are either dark or bright green; the ridged, plated, and attractive bark varies from brown to pale gray; and the hard, heavy, and fine-grained wood is brown.

A few paragraphs ago I mentioned the fact that the Monterey Cypress succeeds under cultivation in various parts of the world. More specifically, people grow it readily in Australia, New Zealand, temperate South America, and southern and western Europe. Here in this country, too, it has been introduced into our southeastern states, and of course it has been heavily planted up and down the Pacific coast—too heavily, some say, with a loss of popular prestige. Yet one would be rash indeed to criticize its value as an evergreen windbreak, screen, hedge, or single specimen.

FREMONT
COTTONWOOD

Just as Palms are identified with the tropics and the Spruces are associated with northern lands, so the Cottonwood belongs to the Central States and the West, at least in the minds of those who know it best. Where other species languish, victims of wind, drought, or what-have-you, Cottonwoods hold their bright, shining crowns high in air above what sometimes seems a poor and inhospitable soil. Through many, many thousands of square miles they mark the winding courses of creeks and rivers and cluster around occasional water holes. Though soft of wood and subject to severe damage by wind in exposed places, they are among the most tenacious of all trees, fast-growing, sprouting freely from below a cut or breakage, and scattering innumerable little seeds far and wide on the wings of the very gales that may have broken them.

The Fremont or Western Cottonwood (*Populus Fremonti*) is a big tree, occasionally 90-odd feet tall and 5 feet thick at the butt. Usually it forms a large, rounded head based on heavy branches, generously spaced, beginning well down on the trunk and forming an interesting pattern that is quite visible even when the tree is in full leaf. In these respects it is typical of many other species of the Poplar tribe to which all the Cottonwoods belong. Ocher-yellow twigs and rather light ashy-brown bark are a pleasant color accompaniment to the smooth yellow-green leaves, beautifully heart-shaped and, because of their form and slender flattened stems, always flickering pleasantly in the slightest breeze; they measure from 2 to 3 inches long and a little more in width. On large trees the trunk bark is deeply and broadly ridged.

The Fremont Cottonwood's native range covers western Texas, southern Colorado, Utah, Nevada, and California, but it now extends considerably beyond this area through introduced plantings. Commercially, it is of considerable importance because of the usefulness of its wood as fuel, in box and inexpensive "gadget" making, and more extensively in the production of wood pulp for the paper industry.

Western Cottonwood, in common with other members of the Poplar clan, reaches a climax of beauty when, in autumn, its leaves turn yellow for a space before loosing their hold and eddying to the ground. The Aspens of the western mountains do the same thing, and for a time the tree life from plains to peaks is bright with golden hues of great beauty. Months ago they had completed their annual task of spreading wee seeds afar in puffs of fluffy white down, and then, with summer fading fast, they seemed to be taking their last cheerful fling of the year.

There are many people who, with some reason, deplore the Cottonwood's untidy habit of scattering its scraps of "cotton" so lavishly during the seeding season. This, though, seems to me a modest price to pay for all the following months of cheerfulness and welcome shade, of resistance to heat and drought, of will and ability to stand up and be counted season after season despite conditions which most trees simply could not face. Furthermore, the "cotton" drawback can be completely banished by making sure that you plant only male trees; it is always the females that produce seeds and their accompanying air-borne sails.

The Western Cottonwood may not be the perfect home-grounds tree—it may, indeed, rather deserve the term "commonplace" sometimes flung against it. But not even its critics can deny the appeal of its shimmering, light-reflecting leaves, its love of life, and its resiliency in the face of adversities. There is much of the flavor of the open spaces in the character of this upstanding tree, something which is good to see and feel.

AMERICAN
HOLLY

Authorities on the early colonial days of the New World know much more about the subject than I do, but I'm willing to guess that when the *Mayflower's* passengers set foot on the Massachusetts coast they found growing there Holly trees so like those they had left behind in England that they must have developed a bad case of homesickness to temper their joy over reaching land at last. For even today the American version of this famous tree still grows wild in that general region, and the similarity between it and its British cousin is so close that one must almost be a botanist to tell the two species apart.

As a matter of fact, there is a strong suspicion among tree people that American Holly (*Ilex opaca*), a few centuries ago, was decidedly more common in the northern states than it is today. We can only speculate as to the reasons for its virtual disappearance, in a wild state, from latitudes north of New York City, with the exception of occasional spots along the Atlantic coast line. Perhaps it was slashed or burned down, perhaps some pestilence of bugs or disease all but wiped it out. I seriously doubt that lack of winter hardiness was a primary factor because (1) occasional Hollies, so old that there seems little likelihood of their having been planted by man, exist in regions far colder than any part of the currently accepted natural range of the tree; and (2) in recent years nursery-grown specimens by the thousand have been planted and firmly established in parts of the North where, according to the popular belief that Holly is a confirmed southerner, they'd simply freeze to death every winter.

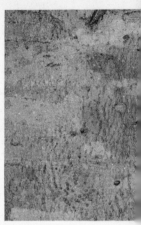

This American Holly is by far the most famous of the nine or so
representatives of the family—about equally divided between trees
and shrubs—which are native to the eastern half of the country.
Generally speaking, it grows wild in sheltered spots and/or near
the coast all the way from Massachusetts to Florida and from southern Indiana south and west to the Gulf and eastern Texas. At its
best it makes a symmetrical, compact tree from 30 to 40 feet tall,
with brownish-gray quite smooth bark covering the tough, close-
grained wood of its trunk. The leaves, of course, are stiff, evergreen,
and tipped with hard semi-spines at the points of their several indentations. Only female trees (all the Hollies are dioecious, which
means that the male, or staminate, flowers are found only on certain specimens, while the pistillate, or female, flowers are restricted
to certain others) can produce berries. Hence, unless a male tree is
sufficiently nearby for insects to transfer some of its pollen to the
female, there just won't be any berries at all. One of the accompanying photographs shows both the male (right) and female
flowers (left) so that you can determine the sex of any specimen
if you happen to see it in blossom.

American Holly is an excellent smallish ornamental tree for a
wide variety of uses on home properties. For its size it gives an
impression of unusual year-round "weight" that make it invaluable

in areas fairly close to the house. As accent points in strategic corners, flanking walk and front entrances, or on or around open terraces, it is in a class quite by itself. Berry-bearing specimens should be given the most important positions, of course, while the essential but non-fruiting males are relegated to spots of less visual importance. Some nurseries are experimenting, I believe, with the idea of grafting a branch from a male tree on a female in order to provide the latter with necessary pollen and thus eliminate the planting of a whole male just for its paternal influence. But to date the ·latter policy is the safest one to follow. One masculine tree, incidentally, is enough to take care of several feminine ones.

Well-drained, comfortably productive soil is best for Holly, despite the fact that in the wild you often find it growing where the soil is sandy and apparently on the poor side. It is a slow-growing tree at best, but it does appreciate a location where its roots can work down to reasonably moist conditions at all seasons. In the North, trees are likely to do better where they are protected from heavy winter winds and get some shade—perhaps for four or five hours of the time that the sun is above the horizon. Early autumn and that period of spring just preceding the start of new growth are the most favorable planting seasons.

Leaf miner is the most troublesome pest, but faithful picking and destruction of infested leaves usually fixes him. If necessary, you can spray the tree with white "summer" oil when the tiny mature insects emerge—May first in New Jersey, earlier farther south.

183

CANOE BIRCH

Oaks for ruggedness and spruces for somber dignity, they say; but the Birch tribe has little use for such sober virtues. Gaiety and grace stand high among its assets, and its bark colors range from bright red-browns down through the silvery grays to the truest white of any American tree. It is in this last category that the Canoe Birch (*Betula papyrifera*) has won its fame and, since long before the Pilgrims landed at Plymouth Rock, has served man faithfully in many ways.

This is the snow-white giant of the north country whose close-textured, waterproof bark has sheathed many, many generations of Indian canoes. Peeled in great sheets from the 2- to 3-foot trunks, shaped and bound with rootlets to springy Cedar or Spruce frames, stitched with more rootlets at the seams and smeared with pitch to seal the joints, the bark was the finest covering material the wilderness could offer man for its own conquest along the water trails. Rolled into a cornucopia, too, and deftly used as a megaphone, it has lured many a bull moose within range of bow or gun, and so resinous and inflammable is it that one could ask for no better material to kindle a campfire. The woods Indians also fashioned various receptacles from it, built tents with it, and even used it in making coffins for the burial of their dead.

The homeland of the Canoe Birch is rich woods and rocky uplands from Newfoundland to the south shore of Hudson Bay, on to the Alaskan coast, and southward into middle New England, the Border States, New York, and northern Pennsylvania. In the northerly parts of this area it is the commonest as well as the most

beautiful of all the Birches, a strikingly effective tree from 50 to 100 feet tall with stout main branches and somewhat irregular form when fully grown. Except for the characteristic blackish scars extending laterally on each side of the branch bases, the bark is chalky white everywhere until you come to the little brown branchlets with their sprinkling of white dots. At all times of the year, but especially during the leafless seasons, this two-tone effect is pleasantly attractive.

Canoe Birch leaves are larger and have more substance than those of other Birches, though their outline and toothed edges conform to the family traditions. They are of a darker, duller green than you find in most other members of the genus, but they yellow pleasantly in autumn. April and May are flowering time, and then a new beauty comes to the tree as the short catkins open and for a time are suffused with soft yellowish tones.

Most of us think of this tree primarily in terms of its bark, whose surface is of such chalklike character that it rubs off easily when it comes into contact with your clothing or skin. Only those who know the Canoe Birch intimately are aware of the fact that the wood underneath the bark is valued too. Close-grained, hard, and tough when properly cut and seasoned, it is a pleasant pale brown with reddish tinges. For many years it has been used for making spools, shoe lasts, wood pulp, and, to a limited degree, as interior flooring and house trim. And, in those regions where the tree grows abundantly, Canoe Birch firewood ranks high.

For some obscure reason the Canoe Birch has never won great popularity as a tree for ornamental planting. It grows rapidly, transplants easily, and is as hardy and vigorous as it is handsome throughout the year. True, it requires considerable space to maintain a normal outline at maturity, but no more than is needed for a Pin Oak, Elm, or any other sizable tree. Besides, in most instances, it is unlikely to reach the same stature under cultivation as it does in its native North Woods where the ground is rich with leaf mold.

Perhaps the fact that it is thought of primarily as a forest dweller, plus its definitely northern range, has worked against its popularity as an ornamental. Actually, south of lower New York State it is unlikely to do well, except in the mountains, however carefully you handle it; presumably it does not like the climate.

COAST REDWOOD

Of all the great trees anywhere in the world, the probabilities are that the most truly titanic are this spectacular evergreen and its close relative, the Giant Sequoia (*Sequoiadendron giganteum*). Three hundred feet tall, nearly 30 feet through the lower part of the trunk, an age limit estimated at 1,400 years—these are the fantastic vital statistics of the Coast Redwood (*Sequoia sempervirens*). Some of its Giant Sequoia cousins are believed to be twice as old. Small wonder that both species are familiar to millions of people as "those big trees out in California."

The history of this amazing evergreen group is as striking as the dimensions of its two living representatives. Away back in the Tertiary period, when our western mountains from Alaska to Panama were being formed, Sequoias grew over a large part of the Northern Hemisphere. More than forty fossilized species have been found, ranging from Italy to Spitzbergen, across Central Asia, and in the western part of our own country. The Petrified Forest of Arizona is a case in point; what we see there today is the record of Sequoias which lived millions of years ago, disappeared beneath a vast ocean, and came to light again in stony form when the present continent rose out of the sea. Only on the Pacific coast, as far as the Western Hemisphere is concerned, did any of the Sequoia group survive the appalling convulsions out of which came the world that we know today. The Redwood here and there in the Coast Ranges of southern Oregon and northern and central California, and the Giant Sequoia on the western slope of the Sierra Nevada range in California—these are all that remain in their full magnificence.

No description can possibly convey the grandeur of a mature Redwood, whether growing alone or in the impressive groves with

which most people associate it. For the record, though, here are some pertinent facts.

To the best of my belief, this species holds the record for being the tallest tree in the world, set by a specimen in Humboldt County, California, with a height of 340 feet; there seems to be some justification for the belief that even taller ones may exist—to 400 feet, perhaps. Many times the trunk is branchless for 100 feet above its flaring base. The bark, from six inches to a foot thick, is ridged and cinnamon brown in color. Inside it the soft, straight-grained wood is crimson brown tinged with gray; it is, of course, of great commercial value for shingles and many other industrial uses.

Most of a Redwood's leaves are from one half to an inch long, very narrow, flat, sharp-pointed, and deep yellow-green. While you might expect the cones to be somewhat in keeping with the tree's own dimensions, they actually are not—only about an inch long and half as broad.

As compared with its close relative, the "Big Tree" of the Sierra Nevadas, the Redwood is far more productive—a most fortunate fact, in view of the overlumbering temptations induced by the commercial value of its wood. It not only produces great numbers of fertile seeds which germinate freely, but it has a habit of sprouting vigorously from the stump after the original tree has been felled. The combined result is that a Redwood forest is liberally provided with strong young growth which, normally, would insure the perpetuation of the species for thousands of years at least. Much of this renewal material, though, is destroyed by the fires which so often follow lumbering operations, so its functioning cannot be taken at full face value.

One might well ask why, if Redwood seeds grow so freely, the species cannot be restored to vast areas where, conceivably, it flourished eons ago. Well, it has been established with considerable success in parts of our southeastern states, and here and there abroad—notably in England. But evidently its potential range is somewhat restricted by climatic conditions; it seems to require not only mild temperatures but also the moisture-laden air found fairly close to the sea.

Theoretically, the preservation of our magnificent Redwood

groves now appears to be legally assured for all time, but let's not be too complacent about that. Commercial interests being what they are, and federal and state governments nowadays being rather unpleasantly susceptible to the power of the almighty dollar when artfully applied by well-organized pressure groups, we will be wise to be constantly on the alert against cleverly cloaked proposals by congressmen and other "representatives of the people" which could easily lead to a return to the almost fatal wastefulness of the past. Only by eternal public vigilance, now and always, can the Redwood forests continue to enjoy the safety which is theirs today—on paper.

JOSHUA TREE

If a specific example were ever needed to demonstrate the gulf that sometimes separates the reasoning of the scientist from the thinking of the layman, I would like to nominate the Joshua-tree (*Yucca brevifolia*) for the job. Look, if you will, at the accompanying photographs and see if you can discover anything lily-like about them— or, for that matter, study a lily blossom out in the garden and try to find even a trace of Joshua-tree in its appearance. Never mind answering, for the truth has already been established by the botanists: both plants are members of the Lily family, believe it or not.

Yuccas—about thirty species, all natives of the Western Hemisphere—are found growing wild in the Southwest, parts of the Deep South, the lower West Coast, and the West Indies. The common Spanish Bayonet of Florida is one, and another is Adam's-needle, hardier than most and an old-time favorite in gardens of the North. Tallest of the lot, and probably the weirdest, is the subject of the present story.

The particular Yucca known as Joshua-tree sometimes reaches a height of 30 feet, the lower half of which is often a comparatively straight and branchless trunk. Once the branches begin, though, they twist and fork and straggle in all manner of odd directions. There are literally no twigs, as we understand the term—just club-like, ungraceful affairs blanketed with dead and drooping old foliage of other years toward the tip tuft of bristly green "leaves." The flower clusters form at the very ends of the branches; they are quite showy heads a foot or more long and somewhat sickishly fragrant. All told, the effect is quite as unorthodox as the desert country where the tree is found from California to Utah, sparsely scattered and seeming entirely in harmony with its surroundings.

The appearance of a young tree is strikingly at variance with that of its parent. For one thing, the youngster is perfectly straight and branchless, and its living foliage is so abundant that the whole

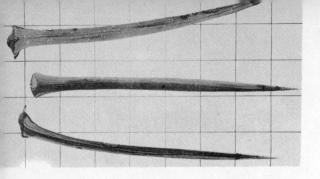

upper half of the trunk almost suggests the bushiness of a fox's tail. The cloak of dead, drooping leaves, too, extends practically to the ground, so that little if any of the true bark is visible. The whole effect is distinctly exotic and rather pleasing, but there is little of the prehistoric impression presented by so many of the mature specimens.

Joshua-tree wood is very porous and soft and is quite useful in paper-pulp making and as packing material. The Indians grind its seeds for meal, too, although this practice is not as common as it once was. In connection with this food angle, it is interesting to note a situation which, I believe, applies to all of the Yucca species:

Investigation has shown that, in the natural state, Yucca flowers are pollinated only through the activities of a small white moth which deliberately gathers the pollen and deposits it in the stigma chamber of the flower. This serves to fertilize the blossom and thereby leads to the formation of seeds, which otherwise would not develop. But here's the catch: the larvae which hatch from the moth's eggs feed exclusively on these same seeds, so that what actually happens might be summarized as:

No moth, no pollen delivery, no seeds; no food for larvae, no future moths, no more pollen placed where it will do any good. In other words, the Joshua-tree must sacrifice very many of its seeds as the price of a few getting a chance to mature and turn into new trees—or into Indian food. And the little white moth makes the Joshua-tree go to work so that the whole procession can keep moving along.

Whence the name Joshua-tree? Well, the story is that the Mormons saw in its fantastic arms a symbol pointing the way to the Promised Land for which they were searching. But one wonders how they decided which limb was the correct one!

WASHINGTON
PALM

The West Coast is abundantly supplied with picturesque trees, but even in a region so notable for horticultural sight-seeing the Washington Palm (*Washingtonia filifera*) is outstanding. Whether growing in the well-kept areas of parks and private estates or in the austerity of its native home among the semi-desert canyons, it is a strange and dramatic blend of beauty and grotesqueness.

Botanically, this is one of two species, both native to North America, which comprise the Washingtonia genus—so named, incidentally, after George Washington. If you look closely at the picture of the single "fan" and the close-up of the trunk, you will see the amazing number of thread-like filaments along the margins of the leaf segments which are responsible for the *filifera* ("thread-bearing") part of the scientific name. The second species, which is credited to Mexico, is *Washingtonia robusta*, a more slender or faster-growing tree with a less uniform "petticoat" of old leaves clinging to its trunk.

This strange tree, like all of the Palms, belongs to a very ancient type of vegetation—as one proof, consider its complete lack of branches as we understand the term. Some specimens reach a height

of 70 or 80 feet and presumably are very old. Normally the actual bark of their trunks is hidden by a heavy thatch of dead, drooping fronds which, barring accidents, extends practically to the ground. Since each frond apparently functions as a living, active part of the tree for about one year, it's easy to see that the thatch on an 80-footer took a long, long time to develop.

Perhaps in a completely unspoiled state of nature this mass of dead brownish growth served some useful purpose in the tree's life, but in the presence of mankind it is a serious fire hazard—people being what they are. Many of the trees in the wild have lost their drapery in a literal blaze of glory, leaving their trunks scorched and scarred. This does not necessarily mean, however, that they have been killed or even seriously injured. In parks and other cultivated areas the "petticoats" are frequently cut off to considerable height in order to lessen this disfiguring fire hazard.

The natural habitat of the Washington Palm is around the borders of the Colorado Desert in California and in southwestern Arizona; it has also been introduced with considerable success along the Gulf coast. Its preference is for alkali soil, and like other Palms, its roots must be able to reach at least a fair supply of water. This is why it is so frequently found near streams and springs.

Apart from their size and odd appearance, Washington Palms are marked by the gray-green color of their living foliage, the numerous 8-inch "threads" already mentioned, and the spray-like clusters of little black fruits which, ripening in September, were once used as food by the Indians of the region.

Palms, as a class, are amazingly useful in the lives of primitive peoples throughout tropical regions, supplying virtually all human needs. Thread for weaving and cordmaking, spines for needles, young shoots for food, sap for wine and sugar, leaves for thatching huts, making hats, mats, and shields, fruits to eat, drink, or press for oil—these are some of the products they have furnished for uncounted centuries. About four thousand species of them are known, girdling the globe. With trunks composed of bundles of long fibers quite different from what we normally think of as wood, they nevertheless possess a strength which enables them to withstand far stronger winds than most regular trees could endure. All are evergreen, and the majority are ever-growing. Some are tree-like, some resemble bushes, others are extensive climbing vines. A versatile clan, indeed, and of them all none is more individualistic, more fantastic in its eye-catching oddity than the subject of this sketch.

199

GRAY
BIRCH

As you look at a well-grown clump of this graceful and justly popular tree, you may well wonder why it was ever named Gray Birch (*Betula populifolia*), for its bark is almost as white as that of its more northern cousin, the Canoe Birch. True, the roughened, nearly black areas at the bases of the branches are larger and usually more numerous than those on the Canoe species, but much of the area between them is virtually white, especially in the sunlight. Perhaps the "gray" idea originated in the fact that not until the tree has gained considerable size does its bark lose the brown-gray tones characteristic of its youth.

The Gray Birch's natural range is from New Brunswick west through New England and New York to Lake Ontario, and southward into Delaware and West Virginia. Throughout this region you find it commonly on wasteland, hill pastures, and rocky slopes, for it is far from particular about soil and actually seems to relish poor, lean land where most other trees would be handicapped if, indeed, they would grow at all. It spreads rapidly by means of tiny double-winged seeds, and loves to take over whole tracts of abandoned fields and clothe them so thickly with its miniature forests that it is no small task to thread your way through them. In spring and summer these big stretches are supremely lovely with their myriads of shining arrow-pointed green leaves. Then, in early fall, the color scheme shifts to buffy yellow as the foliage starts to fall in preparation for those leafless months when the grove will be a symphony of white and gray and lovely red-browns in the bright, cold sunshine.

Gray Birches are comparatively small trees, usually no more than 20 or 30 feet tall and occasionally reaching a height of 35 feet or so

and a trunk diameter of 10 inches. They are definitely slender in form, too, and have few if any large limbs, although there are numerous small ones and a multitude of twigs. The trunks are so thin in proportion to their height that, at maturity, few of them grow straight upward. Instead, the trunks usually lean and bend in subtle curves, partly as a result of wind and their own burden of branches and foliage, but even more as an aftermath of winter ice storms which sometimes bow the trees so that their tops literally touch the ground. If the ice should last for several days, many of the trees will become so "set" that they can never fully recover their normal posture.

Another notable and pleasant characteristic is the tree's habit of developing several trunks from the same root crown—sometimes a half dozen of them more or less alike in length and thickness. The effect is as charming as it is unique, and no doubt is one of the main reasons why the Gray Birch is such a favorite among many, many people throughout our northeastern states.

I wish I could report that this delightful commoner is either durable or long-lived, for it seems a pity that such beauty should not endure for scores of years. Actually, I doubt if any Gray Birch can be expected to last much longer than twenty-odd years, so handicapped is it by its own nature. Besides the storm damage to which its form and rather weak wood condemn it, there is the added drain imposed by the premature loss of its yearly foliage by the attacks of leaf miners which have become common in many areas and, to a great extent, seem to defy human efforts to control them by spraying and other means. Small borers, too, often penetrate the tough, resinous bark and range here and there through the sapwood, operating quite as often among otherwise healthy trees as they do on weakened or crowded ones.

Despite these susceptibilities, I should hate to be deprived of the Gray Birch as an ornamental tree for home-grounds planting. It grows rapidly and transplants readily in early spring, and you can collect your own with little trouble if you dig them when no more than 4 or 5 feet high. Before you realize it, even such babies will be starting to show their typical whiteness, and each year their beauty will increase. And when their course is finally run—well, it's always possible to start afresh.

The best locations, as with nearly all trees, are where the soil is well drained, reasonably productive, and in full sunlight. "Specimen" planting is usually more effective than groupings, for the tree's multi-trunk habit provides its own appropriate company. Few trees are so well adapted to lawn planting, for the Gray Birch is not a voracious feeder, and the shade it casts is too light to have any serious effect on the lawn grass beneath. Finally, as the tree gains in size, it normally loses its lowest branches so that mowing right up to the base of the trunk is an easy matter.

MOUNTAIN HEMLOCK

It was the late Professor Charles S. Sargent, I think, who called this big westerner "the loveliest cone-bearing tree of the American forest." Since Dr. Sargent was not only an outstanding authority on trees but also a New Englander, you can rest assured that his opinion was not tinctured by that shy regional pride which some human residents of our West Coast occasionally display if you push them far enough.

Mountain Hemlocks (*Tsuga Mertensiana*) are well named, for their natural home is at altitudes of 5,000 to 9,000 feet and from the coastal ranges of Alaska southward through British Columbia and California's Sierras, with an extension eastward as far as Idaho and Montana. The tree is especially partial to rugged country, though it must be admitted that the greater the altitude the lower its growth. Thus, in the less exalted portions of its range, it may reach a height of more than 100 feet, with a 3-foot trunk diameter, whereas at the top of its mountain ascent it becomes an almost trunkless, flattened mass of picturesque branches. In writing of the specimens in the Yosemite National Park, John Muir said that some young specimens as tall as 40 feet were bent down by the weight of accumulated snow and completely buried for several months, yet were able to regain their normal position when the white burden melted away under the warming spring sun.

It takes a tough, resilient tree to survive that sort of treatment year after year, and it is no more than natural for large individual specimens to vary considerably in form according to the severity of conditions at the sites which they occupy. Some are rather broad, open pyramids, and these are probably the most normal type. Others, however, are notably irregular and picturesque, like the one shown in the accompanying photograph. But of this you can always be sure: the personality and striking beauty of the tree never flag.

All the Hemlock species have refined, well-tailored foliage, but in the case of the Mountain this asset is especially notable. Its rounded, rather blunt "needles" are so closely packed on the

branchlets that they look almost like small brushes pointing toward the twig where grow the slender 2-inch cones—yellow-green, purplish, or brown, according to their age. These neat-looking little seed holders look so stiff and dry after they have released their cargoes that it is hard to believe that they sprang from strange-looking female flowers shaped somewhat like the tip of one's little finger. And still more unsuspected is the fact that the male flowers, which provide the pollen necessary for seed formation, were forget-me-not blue instead of purple-hued like the females.

In color, form, and general effect the tree's bark is so similar to that of the more widely known Hemlock of the northeastern states (*Tsuga canadensis*) that the family connection is unmistakable. Perhaps the most obvious difference between the two species is the marked tendency of the Mountain's limbs to sweep gracefully toward the ground, in contrast to its cousin's more horizontal or upward-growing habit. On closer examination, too, the needles of the western tree do not present the flattened spray impression that is so characteristic of the easterner. Finally, there are differences under the bark also: close-grained wood in the case of the Mountain Hemlock contrasted with the coarse graining of its better-known relative. In color, weight, and strength of the two woods there is little to choose between them.

It would be a boon to lovers of ornamental trees were the Mountain Hemlock amenable to lowland life in other parts of the country, for its beauty is appealing and unlike that of any other species. But, like many other high mountain plants, it seems unable to adjust itself to less rugged conditions. True, it may live, but its growth will be slow and there is little chance of its ever attaining the picturesqueness that is one of its greatest assets. Your best chance would be to grow it yourself from fresh seed, hoping that the youngsters, never having known the conditions under which their parents grew up, won't miss them too badly. But don't expect too much from them, for generations of high alpine living develop racial peculiarities that are difficult to toss aside. It's just another variation, perhaps, in the old story of too much luxury working evil instead of good on those who are inured to a life of frugality and harsh struggle.

AMERICAN LINDEN

It is very wrong, say the textbooks on How to Become a Writer, to open a story with an apology—it creates a negative impression, alienates the reader's interest, and all that sort of thing. But when one has figuratively lived for years in the shadow of a huge Linden tree, as I did, one is tempted to toss rules into the wastebasket, admit frankly that favoritism is bound to result from such an experience, and then hope that the facts alone will justify one's enthusiasm. Here they are:

If there is such a thing as trees living up to a fine national tradition, the American Linden (*Tilia americana*) does it. Typically it is stately and sturdy, with massive main limbs that build up into a round-topped mass which, while acceptably symmetrical, is never monotonous or lacking in individual character. Seventy-five feet is only moderate height for a well-grown specimen, and an occasional veteran may reach 125 feet with a butt diameter of 3 or 4. Trunk, limbs, and smaller branches are perfectly proportioned, and in late spring the dark red buds on countless outer branchlets burst into more heart-shaped 7-inch leaves than you'd think even so lusty a giant could ever produce. No other American tree casts a denser summer shade and at the same time keeps its central framework so open to the eye. Looking up into a fully foliaged Linden from near its base inevitably suggests a view among the rafters of some mighty tower.

Yet this impressive native of our Middle and Northern States east of the plains has its tiny features, too, as if for pure contrast. In June and July myriad yellowish little flowers, intensely fragrant and practically dripping with nectar, open in small clusters at the tips of curiously bract-like winged stems. Then the honeybees come to the feast from far and near, and for days the air beneath the tree is vibrant with their humming. And finally, long after summer's heat has gone, the old flower stalks give way and, their wings

whirling like propeller blades, spin earthward with their burden of neat, grayish, pea-size seed containers.

The Linden's merit is by no means limited to its value as an ornamental shade tree or its generous output of honey through the medium of the neighborhood bees, for the wood of the trunk and larger limbs plays an important part in our American life. White or pale brown, tough, close, and straight-grained, free of knots and easily worked, it has been used through the generations, under the name of basswood, for making carriage bodies, furniture, woodenware, shoe soles, cooperage, chair seats, charcoal, interior house trim, paper pulp, and fuel. And for more years than you can count, it has been the woodcarver's delight, embodying more of the qualities sought for in this exacting art than are to be found in any other American tree.

I suppose it is too much to ask of any plant that it should have no shortcomings accompanying its many merits, for complete Utopia is as unattainable in the horticultural world as anywhere else. So a fair appraisal of the American Linden must include the fact that its big, soft leaves attract many aphids in midsummer and soon become sticky with honeydew which, catching any dust or smoke that may be in the air, soon turns them unpleasantly dingy. Other insects chew them, too, and high winds shred them until they begin to turn a faded yellow and gradually eddy to the ground. There is no pleasant autumn gold in the Linden's scheme of life, such as brightens the Birches, Tulip Trees, and many others. But, perhaps as a sort of substitute, there emerges once more the full pattern of its enduring framework drawn across the background of the sky.

And what does this big American like in the way of a home? Well, it is definitely at its best in a rich, loamy soil in which its roots can strike deep and range far to find the anchorage, food, and moisture which the complex structure above them must have in order to carry on. But winter cold has no terrors for it, so that even as far north as New Brunswick, Lake Superior, and Manitoba you can count on its staging its months-long show as dependably as it ever did in the old forests of the Ohio Valley where, before the era of destructive lumbering, it was by far the most numerous of the forest trees.

TORREY PINE

This native Californian, whose thick, edible seeds have provided the Indians and Mexicans with food for many generations, is a side-by-side neighbor of the Monterey Pine in parts of the limited area which is the last ancestral home of both species. They are alike, too, in their inability to withstand severe winter cold, but that is about as far as their likeness goes, as comparison of their photographs clearly shows. Specifically, the needles of Torrey are twice as long as those of the Monterey Pine and grow in bundles of five instead of three; its cones are larger and much rougher; and the form of the tree as a whole is more rambling and hit-or-miss.

Most of us, I suppose, think of Pine seeds as being insignificant little characters, sometimes with wings suggestive of those of Maple seeds. But it's a different story with the so-called "nut" Pines, for their seeds are definitely larger and with so much substance that they become worth-while items of human food. Those of the Torrey Pine (*Pinus Torreyana*) are thick and as much as ¾ inch long— almost as large as the seeds of *Pinus longifolia*, from the Himalayas, which probably bears the biggest ones of the whole Pine genus. When you see these seeds at close range, it is easy to understand why they are often called "nuts." The cones which bear them are distinctive too—heavy, woody, and with strong recurving beaks on their scale tips.

Torrey Pines in their native home on Santa Rosa Island and around the mouth of the Soledad River on the neighboring mainland of southern California reach a height of 40 to 60 feet, but under cultivated conditions this latter size may be greatly exceeded.

Unlike the Monterey Pine, the Torrey is not widely used for ornamental planting, perhaps because of its less regular form, possibly for the not infrequent reason that nurserymen have not pushed it into popularity. Despite this lack of acceptance, though, and notwithstanding the extreme smallness of the area to which it is now restricted, the chances of its continued existence for a long time to come seem to be good. Its numerous seeds germinate freely where they fall among the old trees, and the youngsters grow fast and

strongly. Though its back is almost literally to the wall—to the sea, rather—it seems determined to defy the future and keep on going.

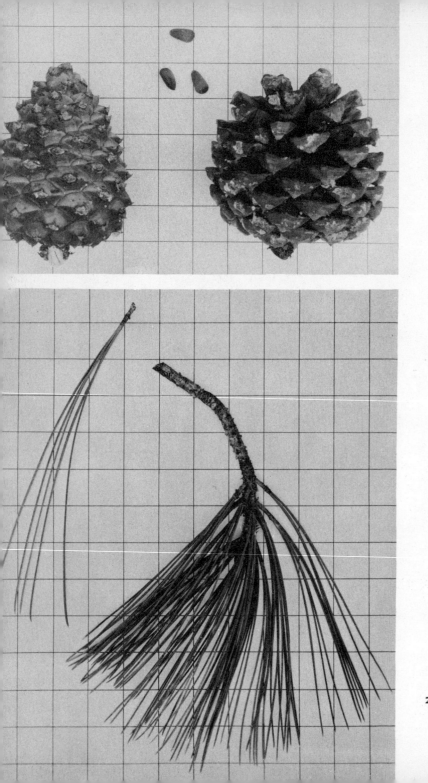

PALO
VERDE

The deserts of our far Southwest are as strangely fascinating as any region you are likely to find in the world. Their moods and impressions are endless, changing even from hour to hour. Sometimes harsh and shimmering under a blasting sun, bright with gaudy bloom, or swept by the softest hues of mauve, purple, and silver, they are a land of infinite subtleties and surprises. But always, wherever you go, you find the patterns of weird plants which, specially equipped to withstand conditions apparently too bitter for any living thing to survive, not only hold their own but would not exchange their hardships for an easier existence if they could.

The Palo Verde (*Cercidium Torreyanum*), high on the honor list of these rugged individualists, is native in California's Colorado Desert, east to Arizona, and southward to Mexico and Lower California. It is a small tree, seldom over 30 feet tall, wide-spreading and densely furnished with branches and twigs which, while slender and graceful, are often armed with stiff, thorn-like spurs. In early spring tiny grayish leaves pop out along these yellowish-green branches, altering their hue for a brief period and then, for reasons best known to nature, loosing their hold and dropping to the ground.

At about this same season, but actually varying from March to June according to the tree's location, clouds of flaring bright yellow blossoms appear, scarcely more than a half inch broad but quite transforming their parent's color effect. And finally come the 2- to 4-inch pea-like pods, whose seeds, fully ripe by midsummer, furnish food for livestock.

The name, Palo Verde, is Spanish and means "green stick." Here, indeed, is the perfectly descriptive title, for until the tree grows very old its entire bark area is green and noticeably smooth. Even when advanced age roughens and grays some of it, green patches still persist here and there as though striving to prove that they're not so ancient after all.

The reason for this pervading and persistent greenness of bark is not fully established, as far as I am aware. It seems reasonable,

however, to credit the theory that in some fashion the bark takes over most of the duty that leaves perform on trees of more conservative habits, which is to help convert the complex chemicals of the sap into usable forms by the presence of chlorophyll and its reactions to light. Certainly chlorophyll is essential to virtually all forms of land plant growth, and there is no doubt that it is invariably green in color. What could be more reasonable than to assume that in this case, at least, it's the bark that really does the job?

This theory gains further support from the fact that the actual leaves, apart from being short-lived and small, are gray rather than green and therefore would seem to be deficient in chlorophyll. The more one thinks about it, the more one suspects that their part in the life processes of the tree is relatively minor.

As to what reasons lie behind such strange provisions—well, I simply cannot guess. Only this much is clear: deserts and all things that live the desert life are tinged with mystery wherever you come upon them. It is as though Nature has set up a battleground to prove that harshness can neither destroy beauty nor be destroyed by it.

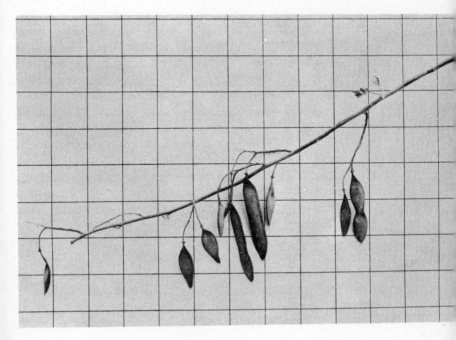

CUCUMBER TREE

Of all the Magnolia species with which we in the United States are familiar, the Cucumber-tree (*Magnolia acuminata*) is probably the hardiest. Its natural range is from western New York, southern Ontario, and southern Illinois down through the Alleghenies into Tennessee, Arkansas, and Mississippi, so you see it can really take cold weather as well as mild, and like them both.

This Cucumber-tree (so called because of the cucumbery appearance of its three-inch fruit with many seeds) is quite a tree. In the mountains of Carolina and Tennessee it occasionally attains a height of 80 or 90 feet and a trunk diameter of 5 feet, though as a general rule it is considerably below these dimensions. When growing in woods it is likely to be on the slender side, a characteristic that applies to most kinds of trees when crowding obliges them to reach upward for the sunlight which they must have. But out in the open, where competition for light is negligible, Cucumber-trees will broaden even to the extent of the one presented on these pages.

All the Magnolias produce showy cone-like fruits containing seeds which, when fully ripe, dangle from curious thread-like connections with those parts of the fruit whence they came. In the case of *Magnolia acuminata* the fruit at first is green, then dull crimson-red, and the seeds themselves are orange-red. All told, this fruiting body adds materially to the tree's ornamental value, especially in years when the number of blossoms has been up to standard. The flowers themselves are not too breath-taking, partly because they are merely a greenish yellow-white, and partly as a result of their moderate size—tulip-shaped and hardly more than 2 inches high. They open toward the end of May.

Its leaves are, as the accompanying photographs suggest, an important ornamental feature of this handsome tree. From 6 to 10 inches long, deep green above and lighter green below, they are thin enough to avoid the semblance of coarseness which their large

size might imply. There are plenty of them, too, for a well-developed tree has very many slender, foliage-bearing branches which, from spring to fall, give substance to the mass effect.

You will like its grayish-brown or sepia-brown bark, too, for on the trunk and main limbs it is surfaced with thin, neat scales in narrow up-and-down ridges that merge into one another as subtly as the currents of a stream.

All told, the Cucumber-tree has much to recommend it as a substantial, rather unusual selection for specimen planting on home grounds of some size. It provides ample shade as well as pleasing appearance at all seasons, and if any of its branches are so low as to interfere with the use of living space within its shade circle, they are easily removed where they join the trunk. It is no more

221

subject to attack by bugs or blights than the average popular ornamental of comparable size—indeed, less so than some. And since its blossoms open so late in the season, they're not likely to be nipped by frost.

Spring, just when the new growth is starting, is the best transplanting time. Even then, though, the work should be done by a good professional if the tree is of any size, for all the Magnolias are rated hard to move. A rich, fairly moist soil is best, and if the location is well away from other trees, your Cucumber-tree will be more likely to do its best, since its roots spread far.

CALIFORNIA
BLACK OAK

For centuries the Oaks have served man conspicuously and in many ways. From their sturdy wood he has fashioned such diverse essentials as quarterstaffs for his protection, timbers and planks for building ships, boards for flooring and furniture making, blocks and plaques for all manner of religious and decorative carving, and odd pieces for literally dozens of other less important purposes. The acorns of certain species were valued food in the old days, the bark provided the best of tannin for the processing of leather, and even today the logs split from trunks and sturdy branches are in steady demand as fuel. These and other facts of practical Oak life are widely recognized, of course. But too little realized is the divergence of size and form among many species.

Esthetically, as you might say, all Oaks are appealing in their ruggedness and picturesque beauty. This single factor, were it their only one, might well put them in the top rank of the "best-loved" class. But actually that is only the beginning of the story.

The California Black Oak (*Quercus Kelloggi*) quite closely resembles the Eastern Red Oak. It is a majestic, broadly domed tree sometimes rising 80 feet or more above the ground, and often its branches are strikingly gnarled in old age. The leaves are smooth and as much as 6 inches long, bright green and borne profusely on stout twigs; their scalloping and notching vary considerably on the same tree, so that for identification purposes the foliage alone is often puzzling. For the last purpose, the acorns are a better clue, since their cups are at least one third as long as the nut, covering much more of it than is the case with Red Oak.

Dark, rough bark with deep valleys and many cross checks is characteristic, and it is exceptionally rich in tannin. The wood beneath it is reddish, coarse-grained, and typically Oak-like, except that often it is too full of pin knots (long-hidden remains of twig growth) to be highly rated for fine lumber purposes. At times there is a decided waviness in the grain that would give it an attractive "figure" were it not for these little flaws.

Springtime is one of the Black Oak's most intriguing seasons, for

it is then that its massiveness is softened by delicate blossom pendants swaying from countless twigs. Their over-all color is a pale yellow-green, varying in tone according to the position of the sun but always incredibly lovely among the pinkish tones of the wee opening leaves. Seeing the tree in this almost fairy-like phase, you can hardly imagine the completeness of the change in its appearance that the ensuing few weeks will bring as the foliage expands and the catkins, having served their pollination purpose, wither and drop to the ground.

This impressive westerner is no less sturdy in its preferred habitat than in its own character. You won't find it near the sea or on the plains, but rather in sunny, open uplands among the mountains throughout California and northward as far as central Oregon. Often it is associated with Firs, Pines, and other typically mountain conifers, and sometimes the even larger California White Oak is among its companions. Seldom, if ever, is it what you could call a real forest tree: it clearly likes the uncrowded groves where small growth is scanty and the big fellows have ample opportunity to expand.

Despite its unquestioned beauty, the California Black Oak apparently is little known outside its native territory. There appears to be no reason why it could not be grown successfully in the Middle Atlantic and lower New England States, as well as southward through the higher parts of Virginia, Tennessee, and North Carolina. I have never seen it in eastern nursery lists and doubt if it could be obtained from such sources.

In view of this situation, you might have to rely on growing your own from acorns, which would involve collecting them yourself or commissioning someone to do it for you. As acorns dry out and lose their power of germination rapidly after falling from the tree, unless they are in contact with soil or some other source of moderate moisture, it is vital they be freshly gathered in autumn and planted within two or three weeks. The best way is to sow them a couple of inches deep and 6 inches apart in well-drained, loamy soil with small-mesh wire laid on top of the area to prevent hungry squirrels or other rodents from digging them out. Seedlings will appear during the following spring and can be transplanted when they have developed four true leaves.

HONEY LOCUST

To say that the Honey Locust (*Gleditsia triacanthos*) is a gentle, friendly sort of tree would be at once misleading and unfair; to assert that it seems hostile and forbidding would be equally far from the mark. The real truth, I suppose, is that it performs the fantastic task of combining all these characteristics so perfectly that it stands as one of the most interesting and likable trees in the whole collection to which this book is devoted. To prove the point we give you a group of intimate photographic studies in which the subject's moods and manners are recorded.

The Honey Locust is a true American which, before mankind introduced it in many more regions, ranged through rich bottom lands from New York and Pennsylvania to Ontario, Michigan, Nebraska, Kansas, and Oklahoma, and south to Georgia, Alabama, Mississippi, and Texas. Today you are likely to come across it anywhere east of the Allegheny Mountains, to say nothing of other parts of the country. Perhaps its finest development is reached in southern Indiana and Illinois, where on occasion it reaches a height of close to 140 feet and a trunk diameter of 2 yards. More usual, though, is a 40- to 60-foot stature, considerably greater than that of the young but typical tree shown here.

Characteristically, the Honey Locust's strong main branches begin to leave the trunk quite close to the ground and, ascending and spreading outward, build the framework of a broad, rather loose but graceful head. Throughout the tree, from trunk to twigs, runs a theme of wiry, independent strength and toughness inherent in the hard ruddy-brown wood that is so enduring in contact with the soil that it has been a favorite material for fence posts ever since men first sought such things in the country round about them.

By all odds the most spectacular feature of this tree is its clusters of thorns or spines that jut from the dark gray bark of trunk and

branches at irregular intervals, forming very practical defenders against climbing creatures that might seek to raid its harvest of enticing young seed pods. Actually these hard reddish-brown spines are modified branches, much more firmly anchored in the underlying wood than are ordinary thorns. Often they are three-pronged, and always they point this way and that, as though to fend off evildoers from any direction. Their maximum length is about 12 inches, and after they reach it they remain firmly in place indefinitely. I know of no other American tree so powerfully prepared to defend itself against invaders.

Despite its rather uncompromising basic character, the Honey Locust changes its over-all effect quite amazingly as the seasons come and go. During the leafless months it looks definitely steely and resilient, like a good fencer poised to attack or momentarily give ground, always parrying and countering his opponent's moves. Then, as spring warms, buds begin to soften the pattern of its twigs with a faintly pinkish haze which presently changes to yellow-green as the young leaves expand. Almost overnight, then, the tree is

transformed by a soft, plumy beauty so delicate that one wonders what can have become of the austerity so apparent only a few weeks ago. Bluish green is the color now, and when a breeze comes the whole tree seems to toss and billow with a sort of carefree abandon that is all but oriental in its richness. By early summer the pendent clusters of inconspicuous greenish flowers open. As their fragrance spreads, the bees gather to the nectar feast, and the sound of their humming is an undertone for the warmth and sunshine and contentment of the day.

Still later, high among the branches, there will be long, twisty seed pods, changing from red and green to shining maroon-brown as they grow toward maturity. While only half ripe, too, they are filled with edible sweet pulp beloved by every country boy. It is from the flavor of this pulp that the tree gets the "honey" part of its name, and deservedly so. Nor is its food fame limited to the younger generation, for it is believed that the "locusts" eaten by John the Baptist in the wilderness were actually the young pods of a European species closely related to our own American tree,

though doubtless the "wild honey" that went with them was just what its name denotes.

These pods are decidedly ornamental features of the tree—more so, indeed, than the flowers. Sometimes they are as much as a foot long and contain a dozen or so small, grayish, bone-like seeds. The pods have their own fantastic note, too, for they cling to the twigs after the leaves have lost their characteristic yellow autumn color, withered, and dropped to the ground. Eventually they fade, and lose their own grip and hurry away on some autumn wind to split and drop their seeds where they may.

Out of all these odd bits of fact, perhaps you can gain some idea of why the Honey Locust is esteemed as an ornamental tree by so many people throughout the areas where it thrives. Its admirers have practical reasons on their side, too, which are well worth considering.

For one thing, it is a sturdy and fairly rapid grower, and even in its early years makes an interesting and distinctive feature. Like most plants, it does best in good soil reasonably well supplied with

moisture, but these conditions are by no means essential; actually it is one of the best drought-resisters I know, and its general tolerance of rather adverse conditions is notable. As you might expect from the nature of its wood and growth, it is long-lived and resistant to storm breakage, for it is a master of the art of yielding just enough to the pressure of strong winds while watching for every opportunity to return to normal position.

From a really long-range viewpoint its potential great size does make it a questionable investment for any except large properties, yet a good many years will pass before it grows too large for places of moderate size. Besides, it stands heavy pruning very well indeed, and that helps greatly in holding it to reasonable proportions. As a matter of fact, a row of young Honey Locusts, planted a yard apart and kept heavily pruned, can be maintained for a long time as a good-sized and extremely distinctive hedge. An opposite extreme, and one which is often recommended, is to plant Honey Locusts as street trees, allowing them to grow to normal proportions and doing only enough pruning to keep their lower limbs out of the way of traffic, pedestrian as well as vehicular.

Tree and shrub nurseries are probably your best source of supply for young Honey Locusts of plantable size. Or, if you don't mind the time involved, you can grow your own from seeds—provided you can find someone who owns a tree that produces them. They're hard little things, but if you soak them in quite hot water to soften their coats a bit before sowing 1 inch deep in the spring, most of them can be expected to sprout before the end of the year.

WHITE FIR

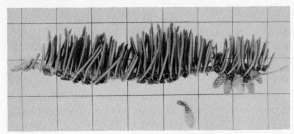

The mountain ranges of the Far West are famed for the vastness of their coniferous forests and the towering heights of the trees which comprise them. Redwood, Douglas-fir, Western Larch, Red Fir, Sugar Pine, Western Hemlock, Lawson Cypress, White Fir—these are giants whose majesty is equaled nowhere else in North America, and but rarely in other parts of the world.

Mountain slopes from southern Oregon through California into Lower California, and from Nevada, Utah, and southern Colorado to Arizona and New Mexico, are the natural range of the evergreen White Fir (*Abies concolor*). It customarily reaches a height of 100 to 180 feet, with an occasional specimen reaching 200 or more because of especially favorable conditions. Its trunk is notably rough and massive, from 3 to 5 feet thick near the butt, and covered with whitish-gray bark, often 6 inches thick and marked with wide, deep furrows. Many years pass before this last condition develops. The bark of young trees is smoother and more of a grayish brown.

Young specimens, also, are definitely pyramidal in outline, like many other conifer species. With advancing age, however, this characteristic gradually disappears and the crowns take on the appearance of rounded cones. This change ushers in the tree's most imposing period, if you are so fortunate as to obtain a good view of one from ground to top, for the less spired top harmonizes with its general massiveness.

For all its rugged size, the White Fir is not without fine beauties. Its leaves, for example, are a pale yellow-green or blue-green, a fact which, in conjunction with the light-colored bark, has led to its other common name of Silver Fir. On the lower branches the individual leaves may be 3 inches long, or twice the size of those near the tree's top. They vary greatly in form, too, as well as in their position on the twig; thus the foliage of a young tree forms flat sprays somewhat after the manner of a Hemlock, whereas there is a strong tendency to curve upward in the case of an older individual. In all cases the needles are blunt, flexible, and arranged in definite ranks.

Another of its minor surprises is the rich red color of the young staminate or pollen-producing cones as you see them ripening on the lower branches in spring and early summer. They are strikingly lovely then, but their show is short-lived, since they die and are shed soon after their pollen has been discharged and some of it carried by air currents to the female cones forming near the top of the tree—a separation of the sexes which, naturally enough, often leads to a scanty seed crop if the weather happens to be unfavorable at the critical time. One wonders, sometimes, why Nature places such obstacles in the path of her provisions for posterity.

The female seed-producing cones grow only on the uppermost branches, where they stand upright instead of hanging head down, as do those of the Spruces. They are from 3½ to 4½ inches long, dull green or sometimes purplish, and ripen in September. One of their oddities is that they do not drop to the ground after shedding their seeds, in the fashion of most conifers. Rather, they practically disintegrate on the tree, losing their scales and then persisting for months as mere rough, ungainly little spikes.

The White Fir's wood has some commercial value as boxing and tub-making material, but it is not the timber tree that some of our other western conifers are. On the other hand, it is valued as a large ornamental and has been extensively planted for this purpose in Europe. The statement that it is the best western Fir for planting in the eastern states is probably true, especially with respect to the form that grows in Colorado. This strain is very hardy, grows rapidly, and is notably resistant to heat and drought. Seedlings of it are reasonably available from some nurserymen, but their Colorado origin should always be specified when ordering. Ultimately all White Spruces become ragged in their old age, but that stage will not be reached for several human generations.

WHITE CEDAR

If you say "White-cedar" to anyone who likes to search out our wild orchids in their native haunts, there's a good chance that his eyes will brighten and he'll rejoin, "That makes me think of the time . . ."—and for the next ten minutes you'll think you are listening to a tropical jungle tale instead of something that occurred perhaps right in your own state. For White-cedars (*Chamaecyparis thyoides*) and some of our loveliest native orchids grow literally side by side in many an extensive swamp along the Atlantic coast from Nova Scotia to Florida, and it is through all but impenetrable wastelands that your true orchid enthusiast flounders with particularly keen anticipation on his exploration trips afield. To make one's way through a real White-cedar swamp is to see at firsthand as perfect an example of nature unspoiled by the hand of man as can be found anywhere in the eastern half of the country.

Though this unsung evergreen is normally a wet-land tree, it succeeds perfectly well in a location where the soil is no more than reasonably damp. Thus it becomes a promising possibility for many home-grounds plantings where its oddly frond-like leafage, quite similar in effect to that of an Arborvitae, will be welcome indeed. It is far from being alone in this matter of liking a change from wet to drier conditions; a number of other swamp trees and shrubs respond in similar manner. Why they rarely try the experiment on their own initiative is not for me to say.

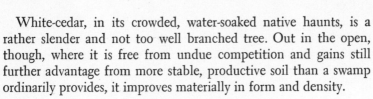

White-cedar, in its crowded, water-soaked native haunts, is a rather slender and not too well branched tree. Out in the open, though, where it is free from undue competition and gains still further advantage from more stable, productive soil than a swamp ordinarily provides, it improves materially in form and density.

Technically, this tree isn't a Cedar at all—indeed, this country has no true Cedars of its own, the representatives of the genus which we do have (chiefly Cedar of Lebanon, scientifically *Cedrus libani*, and *Cedrus atlantica*) being immigrants from North Africa, Asia Minor, or the Himalayas. Probably the application of the common name Cedar to the present tree, and also to our native Redcedar, which is really a Juniper, originated in certain similarities of their wood to that of the real Cedars of biblical fame.

In the northern parts of its range White-cedar seldom reaches a height of more than 40 feet, but in the South it may attain twice that stature and a trunk diameter of 4½ feet. Its wood is close-grained and slightly fragrant, light brown with reddish tinges, and extremely resistant to decay induced by weather exposure or direct contact with soil or water. Few people realize that not long ago, in parts of the low-lying Atlantic coast, there were still in operation what might be called White-cedar "mines"—swamps where, sometimes by quite primitive methods, the buried trunks of great trees that fell centuries ago were excavated and converted into excellent shingles, cabinetmaking material, and long strips for the planking of high-grade small boats. On a number of occasions I have seen samples of this reclaimed wood, and they were in as perfect condition as if they had had only one year of seasoning instead of many hundreds.

Probably the most striking characteristics of this interesting evergreen as far as appearance is concerned are its uniform pyramid or spire form and the feathery delicacy of its massed "leaves." But there is unique appeal, too, in the shredded reddish or grayish-brown bark, used by some kinds of birds for building their nests, and in the strong aromatic scent given off by the foliage when crushed. The cones are tiny—scarcely more than ¼ inch in diameter—and, as a close look at the accompanying photographs will show, they are borne along the stems of the branchlets rather than at their tips.

All in all a distinctive and definitely fascinating tree which, to my way of thinking, should be much better known by far more people. And this one final suggestion: if you are interested in odd and often beautiful wildflowers such as you may never have dreamed of, a real White-cedar swamp is one good place to look for them.

AMERICAN
MOUNTAIN-ASH

Late September in the Taconic Hills of western Massachusetts is a time of subtle golds and blues and fading greens highlighted by the unforgettable flaming-red berry clusters of the Mountain-ash. Here, at elevations of 2,000 feet or so, this striking tree of the North finds its perfect habitat and setting on the rocky, wooded slopes amid small Oaks, Maples, and Chestnut saplings springing from the roots of an all but extinct race that once dotted these hills with mighty trunks and rounded crowns towering above all the rest. Often, from the higher trails, one looks directly down into the top of a Mountain-ash growing in a ravine below and spreading its beauty like a billowing carpet in the sunlight.

This American Mountain-ash (*Sorbus americana*) is by no

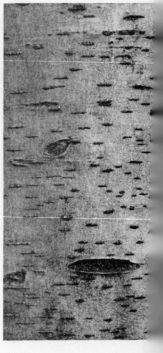

means a large tree; seldom does it exceed 30 feet in height, and perhaps 15 to 20 feet better defines its normal stature. Definitely it is refined in character, with rather smooth gray-brown bark, slender branches, and small compound leaves, red-stemmed and with a grace peculiarly their own. The fruits, perhaps its greatest glory, follow the flat-topped white flower clusters of May and early June.

Its normal range is from Newfoundland west to Lake Winnipeg (in Manitoba) and south to Connecticut, northern and western New York, the Great Lakes region, and down through the Alleghenies into North Carolina. Thus, clearly, it is a cool-country species and by no means to be confused with its quite similar but somewhat more adaptable cousin the European Mountain-ash (*Sorbus aucuparia*), the famous Rowan Tree so often mentioned in the poetry and prose of England. The European species, incidentally, is often offered by nurserymen over here.

I have dwelt at some length on the native habitat of this tree as a means not only of suggesting its beauty but also to emphasize the fact that its successful adaptation to home-grounds planting is by no means a country-wide matter. Outside of its cool natural range the American Mountain-ash rarely does well and is discouragingly subject to injury, and even death, at the hands (or jaws!) of the roundheaded apple-tree borer, its most serious insect enemy. This pest poses an especially difficult problem, for it is very hard to bring under control once it gets started.

There was a time not long ago when the scientists called this tree *Pyrus americana*, which clearly grouped it with the pears. Further botanical study, however, resulted in its being transferred to its present genus. But even that does not explain the "Ash" part of its common name, for the true Ashes are still something else again, with slender winged seeds instead of round, berry-like fruits. It's all very confusing indeed.

On the whole, I like our native Mountain-ash best when it is growing in naturalistic surroundings—perhaps at the edge of a clearing or on a wooded slope where the other trees are neither so large nor so dense as to block out the sunlight which it needs for best development and display. Somehow it seems most at home in such settings, but I'm sure that in any place where it will grow you'll like it.

PIGNUT
HICKORY

In the minds of born-and-bred country people the characteristics and associations of certain trees often endow them with personalities as well defined as those of human beings. Somber or gay, delicate or rugged, friendly or aloof—much of your impression of some tree over the years is keyed by the circumstances under which you first came to know it well.

In view of this situation, I suspect that the rather lowly common name of the Pignut Hickory (*Carya glàbra*) originated in a scornful attitude toward the eating quality of its nuts as compared with those of its closely similar cousin, the Shagbark Hickory. Generation after generation of country kids grew up to despise the flavor of those sometimes thick-shelled, always thin-husked little nubbins; pigs might like it, but pigs'll eat 'most anything!

Yet this maligned but sterling tree has many, many friends in the back country. Its wood is almost identical in strength, springiness, and appearance with that of the more famous Shagbark, and just as useful for just as many purposes. The two trees grow to roughly equal size (sometimes 120 feet or more), resemble each other in general appearance except that the Pignut's bark is dark gray and less shaggy than the Shagbark's light gray overcoat, and their natural ranges are about the same—from southern Maine westward into Nebraska, down south to Texas, Alabama, et cetera. Their local preferences differ, though, for whereas the Pignut likes dryish, rocky woods, the Shagbark is more often found where the soil is rich. Both kinds demand good drainage.

The Pignut is a rough-and-ready countryman, sturdy of root and branch, indifferent to the rigors of harsh weather, a plain fellow as realistic as the hills on which he grows. Coarse of leaf and irregular of bark, he would look as out of place on a sophisticated lawn as a farm boy walking down Fifth Avenue. Without crows to perch in his leafless autumn crown and squirrels to scurry up and down his trunk, I fear he'd never feel quite right. The place to know and love him is back among the hills where, generations ago, he thrust his first leaves upward from a commonplace little nut, even as his parents and his parents' parents did in their time.

Botanically speaking, the Pignut Hickory has what are known as compound leaves—several of them along a central stem whose base is connected to the true twig in much the same manner as the stem of an ordinary single leaf. The leaflets (individuals which comprise the group) usually are five or seven in number, the largest one at the tip being about 7 inches long. Their characteristic color is a deep yellow-green which turns more yellowish in autumn before the leaves shrivel and drop.

The roughness of the bark develops only after the tree has reached some size, and even then the branches retain their smoothness. Evidently the rough character is just a matter of age, but even a sapling no more than an inch or so thick gives notice of what will happen later.

Pignuts, like other Hickories (a strictly North American tribe, by the way), have two types of flowers—male and female. The former, which are in the form of flexible greenish-yellow catkins several inches long hanging in clusters near the twig tips, provide the pollen for the group of much less conspicuous female blossoms borne at the very end of the twig.

Apart from its flowers, though, a Pignut puts on quite a beauty show when its big buds drop their outer scales in spring and, growing thick and longer, finally shake out their bundles of pale green leaflets. At this stage the large, almost petal-like inner scales turn back and for a short time make the branches look as if they were dotted with the softest of green, orange, and pale buff blossoms.

The husk which encloses a Pignut's nut is much thinner than usually thought of in connection with other trees of the genus. Also, it is unlikely to split more than halfway down, and often the nut, fully ripe, drops from the tree while still inside its outer covering. The complete fruit varies considerably in size and shape, for

this particular Hickory seems to be less fixed in physical details than the rest of its cousins. You can always expect the nuts themselves to have a brownish cast, however, with a fine little network of light-colored marks.

All Hickories, unfortunately, are subject to damage by a variety of borers, beetles, aphids, and galls, which can be controlled reasonably well if you can get at the tree with power spraying apparatus at the right times. The most spectacular of its enemies is a huge, fearsome-looking spiny caterpillar known as the horned devil—an appropriate but inadequate name for a character whose mere appearance is so unpleasant as to keep you awake nights unless you are shockproof to crawling monstrosities. It seems odd indeed that trees with wood of such abiding hardness and closeness of grain even when green should fall victim to soft-bodied, tough-jawed grubs that chew their way into it with apparent ease; but facts are facts.

Index

INDEX

A

Abies concolor, 233
Acer
  rubrum, 33
  saccharinum, 35
  saccharum, 35, 101
Aesculus
  californica, 162
  hippocastanum, 155
Ash
  Mountain. *See* Mountain-ash
  White, 72

B

Bay
  Bull, 20
  California. *See* California-laurel
Beech, American, 24
Betula
  papyrifera, 184
  populifolia, 200
Birch
  Canoe, 184
  Gray, 200
Buckeye. *See also* Horse-chestnut
  California, 162
Buttonball. *See* Sycamore
Buttonwood. *See* Sycamore

C

California-laurel, 168
Carya
  glabra, 243
  ovata, 76
  pecan, 97

Cedar
  Incense. *See* Incense-cedar
  Red. *See* Red-cedar
  White. *See* White-cedar
Cercidium Torreyanum, 216
Chamaecyparis thyoides, 236
Cornus florida, 136
Cottonwood, 148
  Fremont, 178
Cucumber Tree, 220
Cupressus macrocarpa, 175
Cypress, Monterey, 175

D

Diospyros virginiana, 112
Dogwood, Flowering, 136
Douglas-fir, 132

E

Elm, American, 116

F

Fagus sylvatica, 23
Fir
  Douglas. *See* Douglas-fir
  White, 233
Fraxinus americana, 72

G

Gleditsia triacanthos, 227
Gum
  Black. *See* Pepperidge
  Sour. *See* Pepperidge
  Sweet, 46

H

Hemlock, 80
  Carolina, 82
  Mountain, 204
  Western, 82
Hickory
  Pignut, 243
  Shagbark, 76
Holly, American, 181
Horse-chestnut, 155

I

Ilex opaca, 181
Incense-cedar, 165

J

Joshua Tree, 192
Juglans nigra, 91
Juniper, Western, 124
Juniperus
  occidentalis, 124
  virginiana, 28

L

Laurel, California. *See* California-
      laurel
Libocedrus decurrens, 165
Linden, American, 208
Liquidambar styraciflua, 47
Liriodendron tulipifera, 83
Locust
  Black, 65
  Honey, 227

M

Magnolia
  accuminata, 220
  grandiflora, 20
Magnolia, Large-flowered, 20
Maple
  Red, 33
  Sugar, 101
Mountain-ash, American, 239

N

Nyssa sylvatica, 121

O

Oak
  Black, 105
    California, 223
  Live, 172
    California, 128
    Coast, 128
  Northern Red, 50
  Pin, 88
  White, 62
  Willow, 152
Oregon-myrtle. *See* California-
      laurel

P

Palm, Washington, 196
Palo Verde, 216
Pecan, 97

Pepperidge, 121
Persimmon, 112
Picea
  mariana, 69
  ponderosa, 157
Pine
  Long-leaf, 144
  Monterey, 17
  Ponderosa, 158
  Sugar, 41
  Torrey, 212
  White, 59
Pinus
  Lambertiana, 42
  palustris, 146
  radiata, 17
  strobus, 59
  Torreyana, 212
Plane-tree. See Sycamore
Platanus occidentalis, 37
Poplar
  Carolina, 148
  Yellow. See Tulip-tree
Populus
  canadensis, 148
  deltoidea, 148
  Fremonti, 178
Pseudotsuga taxifolia, 134

Q

Quercus
  agrifolia, 128
  alba, 62
  borealis, 50
  chrysolepis, 128
  Kelloggi, 223
  palustris, 89
  phellos, 153
  velutina, 105
  virginiana, 130, 172

R

Red-cedar, 28
Redwood, Coast, 108, 188
Robinia pseudoacacia, 65

S

Sassafras, 54
Sassafras variifolium, 54
Sequoia, Giant, 108, 188
Sequoia sempervirens, 188
Sequoiadendron giganteum, 108, 188
Sorbus americana, 239
Spruce, Black, 69
Sycamore, 37

T

Tilia americana, 208
Tillandsia usneoides, 172
Tsuga
  canadensis, 80
  mertensiana, 204
Tulip-tree, 83
Tupelo. See Pepperidge

U

Ulmus americana, 116
Umbellularia californica, 168

W

Walnut, Black, 91

253

Washingtonia
    filifera, 196
    robusta, 196
White-cedar, 236
Whitewood. *See* Tulip-tree

Y

Yucca brevifolia, 192